Alcoholic Thinking

ALCOHOLIC THINKING

Language, Culture, and Belief in Alcoholics Anonymous

DANNY M. WILCOX

Westport, Connecticut
London

Library of Congress Cataloging-in-Publication Data

Wilcox, Danny M., 1950–
    Alcoholic thinking : language, culture, and belief in Alcoholics
    Anonymous / Danny M. Wilcox.
        p.   cm.
    Includes bibliographical references and index.
    ISBN 0–275–96049–8 (alk. paper)
       1. Alcoholism—Psychological aspects. 2. Alcoholics Anonymous.
    3. Recovering alcoholics—Psychology. I. Title.
    HV5045.W55   1998
    362.292′86—dc21   97–34740

British Library Cataloguing in Publication Data is available.

Copyright © 1998 by Danny M. Wilcox

Library of Congress Catalog Card Number: 97–34740
ISBN: 0–275–96049–8

First published in 1998

Praeger Publishers, 88 Post Road West, Westport, CT 06881
An imprint of Greenwood Publishing Group, Inc.

Printed in the United States of America

The paper used in this book complies with the
Permanent Paper Standard issued by the National
Information Standards Organization (Z39.48–1984).

10 9 8 7 6 5 4 3 2

Copyright Acknowledgments

The author and publisher gratefully acknowledge permission to use the following material:

Excerpts from *Alcoholics Anonymous*, third edition, New York: Alcoholics Anonymous World Services, 1976; and *The Twelve Steps and the Twelve Traditions*, New York: Alcoholics Anonymous
World Services, 1981. These excerpts are reprinted with the permission of Alcoholics Anonymous
World Services, Inc. Permission to reprint the excerpts does not mean that A.A. has reviewed or
approved the contents of this publication, nor that A.A. agrees with the views expressed herein. A.A.
is a program of recovery from alcoholism *only*; use of the excerpts in connection with programs and
activities which are patterned after A.A., but which address other problems, or in any other non-A.A.
context, does not imply otherwise.

Excerpts from *AA Grapevine*, New York: AA Grapevine, 1947. Copyright © by the AA Grapevine
Inc.; reprinted with permission.

To Those Who Suffer

Contents

Acknowledgments

I first became aware of Alcoholics Anonymous (AA) while attending meetings as a court mandated observer. Subsequently, I voluntarily returned to AA in an effort to deal with my own specific problems with alcohol. The research that this book is based on grew directly from that involvement. However, I want to make absolutely clear that I am not currently an AA member. I have the utmost respect for the Twelve Traditions of AA, including the principle of anonymity at the public level and would do nothing to violate the essential principles of the organization. Nor should anyone ever suggest that I am an AA spokesperson or that I represent AA in any capacity. This is a research report based on the experience of many people in AA, as well as my own, but it is important to remember that AA does not sanction this book or any underlying studies. In fact, AA as an organization is not interested in supporting any type of research. The single organization's purpose is to help alcoholics to achieve and maintain sobriety. These traditions have provided great strength and direction to the organization for over sixty years. I want to make clear that the presentation of the material and the conclusions of this study are strictly my responsibility.

It is difficult to express my debt to Jack and Irene Wilcox, my father and mother. I thank my wife, Linda Anne, for her support in making this work a reality. To family members and to those who have suffered my endeavors over the past 20 years, I beg forgiveness and offer my deepest love and appreciation. To the many members of Alcoholics Anonymous who made this research possible, I owe my sober state of life. I thank H. Gill-King for initiating my interest in Anthropology, my many teachers and colleagues, for sustaining it, and Bill Pulte for improving the manuscript. Special thanks go to many others. I want to thank the University of North Texas and the faculty of the Institute of Anthropology for the important support, which helped me to complete and publish this work. Finally, I want to express my gratitude to my friends, Kenny Moore, Rick Flora, Jesse Smith, and Gary Kent.

Introduction

Alcohol is a drug. Unlike other drugs, it is available to anyone of legal age and easily acquired. Two out of every three Americans over age 18 use some alcoholic beverage. Most of these 120 million people are social drinkers and consider their right to drink as inalienable as "life, liberty, and the pursuit of happiness." Americans are encouraged to drink. Many businesses depend heavily on alcohol sales. Sports centers, restaurants, drinking establishments, and the beverage and advertising industries all have a serious economic stake in the acceptance of alcohol. But every American that pays taxes or a monthly premium for health insurance has an equally important interest in the 10 percent of the adult population that exhibit symptoms of alcohol dependence or habitual abuse.

The National Institute of Alcoholism and Alcohol Abuse (NIAAA) estimates that more than 11 million adults in the United States are alcohol dependent and another 7 million regularly abuse alcohol. These 18 million individuals and others unlucky enough to suffer from single bouts of drinking contribute 16 billion dollars per year to health care costs. Approximately 20–40 percent of all hospital beds are occupied by someone with an alcohol-related problem, 20–45 percent of all homeless people are alcohol impaired, and alcohol is a contributing, causal factor in 3 percent of all deaths.

Alcohol is the most prevalent drug problem in America today. At a total cost of 150 billion dollars per year, it is also the most expensive. The American public pays the bill as millions of people struggle with dependence on alcohol. Most alcoholics fight their battle alone. They live in increasing isolation and attempt to juggle survival and contentment while becoming progressively debilitated by the excessive use of alcohol.

Alcoholics Anonymous (AA) is a mutual-help organization of almost 1 million members in the United States and other countries. Most of them claim it is effective in fostering, effecting, and maintaining recovery from alcoholism. The 12-step program of AA has been adapted to the treatment of other addictions like eating, smoking, gambling, and sex. Still, the general population and the academic community are sceptical and misunderstand the nature of the organization and its effectiveness as treatment.

Based on the author's 13 years of experience as a practicing alcoholic, his training as an anthropologist, and observation and participation at over 600 AA meetings, *Alcoholic Thinking: Language, Culture, and Belief in Alcoholics Anonymous* demonstrates for the first time that an individual doesn't have to be a practicing alcoholic to think like one. Anyone can be victimized by alcoholic thinking; then just add the alcohol. Chapter 1 sets the object of the study, Alcoholics Anonymous, within the interdisciplinary study of alcoholism over the past 50 years. Chapter 2 explores the development of the alcohol focus in anthropological work and the method of investigation used in this study. Chapter 3 describes how people affilliate with AA, and Chapter 4 offers a detailed description and analysis of the ritual and ceremonial quality of the AA meeting. Chapter 5 represents the 12-step program of AA in the context of other folk healing practices, and Chapter 6 shows how the specialized language shared through AA culture fosters a change in thinking and worldview that is critical to the process of recovery. Finally, Chapter 7 explains how the development and practice of alcoholism is an integral and presently unavoidable aspect of American culture.

The narrative is written in a straightfoward, readable style yet is well referenced and retains a discussion of the issues that can be appreciated by specialists. In contrast to most published work about Alcoholics Anonymous, this book is not primarily directed to a recovery audience. The NIAAA estimates that three or four people are directly touched by the negative consequences of each person suffering from alcoholism or alcohol abuse. Studies have consistently shown that dependence often manifests itself as a family disorder. Daily news in print and broadcast media reflect a growing awareness of the far-reaching effects each alcoholic has on others. Of the 70–80 million Americans who are profoundly affected by alcohol, those who seek to identify the problem and find a potential solution to benefit themselves, boyfriends, girlfriends, spouses, offspring, family, and friends will find the book helpful. It will assist employers in recognizing how alcohol problems quietly restrict productivity and to identify the type of support necessary for recovery. The description is intended to inform researchers and lay persons alike who have little or no direct experience with AA about the structure, methods, and theory of the organization, groups, and individual members.

People concerned about their own relationship with alcohol will find the approach appealing. Only about 5–7 percent of alcoholics are members of AA. For each person who recovers, 18 or 19 others reject or won't consider participating despite problems with alcohol. These and other drinkers will be curious to encounter a critical analysis that seeks to explain alcohol dependence and recovery as a cultural rather than a strictly personal phenomenon.

Those interested in addiction and recovery literature will perceive the book as quite different from the mainstream. Even though it presents language and concepts evident in recovery work, this book takes a unique view of Alcoholics Anonymous as a discrete cultural entity. Most readers will find the emphasis on shared community values and the explication of AA as a cultural system, a new and exciting perspective. Professionals engaged in the interdisciplinary study and treatment of alcoholism will discover the only accurate, extensive, ethnographic description of the culture of Alcoholics Anonymous. Such a study has been absent, but needed. This book is meant to be an irreplaceable, though controversial academic resource for researchers and teachers of courses at all levels concerning the development, practice, and recovery of alcoholics.

Researchers have done a tremendous job in explaining causes, practice, and recovery. Their work is critically valuable, but somewhat clinical and distant. It is generally restricted to academic and professional markets. On the other hand, many experienced and involved alcoholics and addicts have produced an important body of work. Many of these efforts are extremely thorough when presenting the predicament and possible solutions, but usually they are directed at a recovering audience. *Alcoholic Thinking* combines the views of experienced insiders with behavioral analysis based in competent social science. It is a descriptive analysis of the recovering alcoholic's culture in AA. Through the perspective of alcoholism as a cultural process that affects the way people think about themselves and others in relation to the world, this book investigates how and why people become alcoholic. It also answers why and how they can recover by changing the way they think and seeking a new conceptual awareness of themselves and the world around them. The incessant human longing to understand the world as a mysterious creation and a spiritual journey is reflected in much popular nonfiction and fiction today, as well as being a traditional human perspective on reality since ancient times. This ethnography of the language, culture, and beliefs of recovering alcoholics in AA reflects how one group of troubled people make their own spiritual journey from sickness to health.

1

Alcohol Use in America

PREVALENCE OF ALCOHOL USE

Alcohol is the most widely used drug in the United States, surpassing even tobacco (NIAAA 1990). Approximately two thirds of the entire population over the age of 18 consumes some form of alcoholic beverage (Hartford and Parker 1985). The vast majority of these individuals are "social drinkers." They seem to suffer no ill effects as a consequence of their drinking, nor do they have any problems discontinuing the use of alcohol. In fact, they may derive a great deal of enjoyment from sharing a drink at parties, weddings, and other celebrations, having a cocktail with friends or business associates, stopping to grab a six-pack after a hard day's work, or drinking a bottle of fine wine with an intimate friend at dinner.

Alcohol is everywhere. It is readily available at liquor, convenience and grocery stores, baseball parks, football stadiums, basketball games, golf courses, restaurants, clubs, bars, and many other places. It can be acquired if you have the money and an identification card that proves you are over the required legal age. It is an integral part of entertainment for a large segment of the population and, as long as it is used in the appropriate manner, it usually enjoys general acceptance. As the attempt at prohibition in this country demonstrated, many consider the use of alcohol to be as much an inalienable right as "life, liberty, and the pursuit of happiness."

Some people are introduced to alcohol use by their parents or relatives. Others, whose parents would never dream of putting a drink in front of their adolescent, and sometimes younger children, share their first drinking experiment with friends "just to see what it's like." Very few young people in the country escape at least one such experiment. In a 1988 survey, 92 percent of high school seniors were found to have tried alcohol and approximately two thirds described themselves as current drinkers. Half of those who claimed to be current drinkers characterized themselves as heavy drinkers (Johnston et al. 1988) despite the recent development of new attitudes and beliefs that reflect greater awareness of the hazards of alcohol use.

Most Americans begin to learn about alcohol very early in life. Children of parents who use alcohol begin to observe this behavior long before they are allowed to drink, and many have observed children crying to their mother, father or sibling that they "want some, too." Many parents tire of the child's incessant whining and give them some to "shut 'em up." Not many would argue that young children are too innocent to comprehend the obvious changes in behavior that result from various levels of alcohol intoxication. From these behaviors they also begin to learn what is acceptable or prohibited while drinking.

PRESSURES TO DRINK AND THE PROFITS OF ALCOHOL

Adolescence brings not only pressure from peers to experiment with alcoholic beverages, but the individual is bombarded with suggestions from the beverage industry (Atkins 1987). Billboards along the highways are plastered with countless messages that some type of alcohol is available, and often this basic information is supplemented with the image of a sexually attractive young person. The image of glamorous sexuality is also frequently exploited in many television commercials and much programming (Rychtarick et al. 1983, Wallack et al. 1987). A 20 or 30 minute drive home on the freeway, and an evening in front of the television make perfectly clear why most self-described "heavy" drinkers are young, male, and unmarried (Hilton 1987). The beverage industry has decided these messages are effective or they wouldn't allocate such incredible resources to advertising, as well as lobbying government representatives to obtain favorable rulings that might well affect the availability of such messages.

Young adults fortunate enough to go to colleges or universities have the opportunity to engage in serious "on-the-job training" if they have been deprived of such drinking experience previously, although at least one college administrator seems to think that most freshmen come fully trained (Marvel 1993). If they don't already know by the time they begin college, they learn that just about everybody drinks, has a good time, and that it is the norm. Young people fortunate enough to enter the work force find many opportunities to share the fun of "having a few" at quitting time with their co-workers. As these young people involve themselves with drinking, they also further the knowledge they have already garnered from people, television, advertising, movies, and books. These social occasions provide them the opportunity to experience the extended limits of expected behavior when drinking. They have been enculturated into a behavioral system that is based on expected rules of conduct, and they learn that these rules change a little if they are drinking (MacAndrew and Edgerton 1969).

The beverage industry, restaurants, drinking establishments, and sports centers all over the country have a serious economic stake in the acceptance of drinking for entertainment, and it is extensively promoted. Despite the fact that alcohol can have serious physical, social, and personal effects, which are detrimental, it is regarded as a harmless social necessity by most individuals. The fact that even single bouts of drinking can constitute high-risk behavior is generally overlooked. While many parents, friends, family and professionals warn of the dangers of other drugs, they feel that alcohol is okay. After all, "it wouldn't be legal if it wasn't."

ALCOHOL PROBLEMS IN CONTEMPORARY AMERICAN SOCIETY

For those individuals who cannot confine themselves to social drinking and abuse alcohol or become alcohol dependent, the dangers are evident. Although alcoholic beverages are legal and encouraged by general social acceptance, the effects of consumption constitute one of the most persistent problems in American society. Alcohol has been associated with liver disease, pancreatitis, gastric and esophageal cancer, exacerbation of peptic ulcers, various neurological disorders, anemia, profound effects on carbohydrate, lipid, and protein metabolism, cardiac dysfunction, hypertension, and effects on immune, endocrine, and reproductive functions. Furthermore, fetal alcohol syndrome is one of the leading causes of mental retardation and can be totally prevented simply by not drinking when pregnant (NIAAA 1990).

Nearly half of all accidental deaths, suicides, and homicides of males under 34 years of age are associated with alcohol use (NIAAA 1990). It is a contributing factor to over 20,000 traffic fatalities per year and these victims are frequently young (Baker et al. 1984). Suicide victims are more likely to be alcohol dependent or to have been drinking just prior to killing themselves (Rozien 1982, Colliver and Malin 1986). Homicides are frequently committed while under the influence. It has also been estimated that between 20–45 percent of all homeless people are in some way alcohol impaired (Mulkern and Spence 1984, Wright et al. 1987).

Alcohol has been estimated to be a contributing, causal factor in at least 3 percent of all deaths in the United States (Van Natta et al. 1984–85). The medical complications of alcohol use, abuse, and alcoholism cause affected persons to spend much more on general health care (Holder 1987) and contribute as much as 16.5 billion dollars to additional health care costs each year (Harwood et al. 1985). Additionally, it is estimated that at any given time 20–40 percent of all hospital beds are occupied by someone with an alcohol related problem (NIAAA 1990). Many accidents and much trauma sustained by assault, by attempted suicide and homicide are the result of single bouts of drinking. This fact should not be easily overlooked by the casual, social drinker when assessing the very personal risks associated with alcohol consumption. But the vast majority of the problems described are the result of consistent alcohol abuse and chronic, prolonged use by the alcohol dependent individual.

Alcoholism is the most prevalent drug problem in the United States. Everyday millions of people struggle with dependence on alcohol. Often, they lose their jobs and the ability to care for their families. Abuse, neglect, poverty, domestic violence, and broken homes are a frequent result. Sometimes they lose the ability to care for themselves and augment the legion of homeless people in the country. A large segment of the prison population was alcohol dependent or abusing alcohol at the time of offense. All these things, combined with the sheer number of car crashes, falls, burns, and other accidental injuries or fatalities to which the use of alcohol contributes, not only create demands for various types of local, state, and federal assistance, but also require individuals and institutions to allocate considerable resources to deal with the problem. Alcohol is not only the most prevalent drug problem in the country, but at an estimated total cost in excess of 150 billion dollars per year, it is the most expensive (Harwood et al. 1985).

These examples represent the most extreme problems associated with alcohol dependence. Far more people manage to maintain their households and themselves in such a way as to continue a somewhat productive lifestyle but at a real cost to themselves and to those around them, which often becomes an increasing burden. Employers suffer considerable losses in productive capacity. Families suffer the loss of affection and financial assets, which may not seem significant for many years but which ultimately leads to serious problems.

A relatively few people who suffer from alcoholism become aware of their dependency on alcohol and become involved in various treatment programs. Many of these people do recover and once again begin to lead more productive lives. Survival rates for those in recovery are much greater than those who continue to drink. Many alcohol dependent people fail and abandon the recovery process. "Those who do relapse and continue to drink . . . not only face greater difficulties with family relationships and with physical and psychological health, but are more likely to die. While they live they are more likely to suffer from depression and anxiety, to use medications, to have been hospitalized, and to smoke tobacco and have more related problems" (Finney and Moos 1991: 52). They continue to suffer even though they may be able to manage their lives on a somewhat productive basis.

The National Institute of Alcohol Abuse and Alcoholism (NIAAA) estimated in 1990 that approximately 10 percent of the adult population in the United States exhibits symptoms of alcohol abuse or dependence. In 1990 there were approximately 10.5 million alcohol dependent people in this country and another 7.2 million who abuse alcohol on a regular basis, although they do not show symptoms of dependence. The number of alcohol dependent individuals was expected to reach 11.2 million by 1995 while the number of alcohol abusers was expected to remain the same (NIAAA 1990). Considering the problems associated with these types of drinking patterns, and that many individuals are not completely unaware of the consequences, these estimates are astounding.

Critical studies regarding general problems of the society with respect to health care, divorce rates, malnourished and abused children, lost jobs, wages and families, and productivity, judicial backlogs, violence, prison overcrowding, and accidental injury and death are important. But the very nature of alcoholism, its effects on the individual who suffers, the decaying quality of the lives of most alcoholics, and the possibility of recovery deserves close examination as well.

The Seventh Special Report to the U.S. Congress on Alcohol and Health states that research should be "aimed at determining the reasons that people drink, the reasons they continue to drink even though alcohol use creates problems for them, and the reasons that some are unable to stop drinking even in the face of highly detrimental outcomes" (NIAAA 1990: 1). By using an anthropological perspective and method, this study will look specifically at the "reasons" that perpetuate the problem of alcoholism in the United States today. Although there are many different treatment alternatives available to the alcohol dependent individual, this study will look specifically at Alcoholics Anonymous as one solution to the problem.

FOLK CONCEPTS OF ALCOHOLISM

As Americans, we all think we know an alcoholic when we see one. The bums begging on the street are alcoholics. You can tell just by looking at them. They are weak willed, morally inadequate people who don't give a hoot about anything but their next drink. They start drinking in the morning and drink all day. They love to drink and they live to drink. They are hopeless and they are probably going to die on skid row. We all know about the working man who gets drunk every day after work and goes home and beats his wife. We know about movie stars and famous people who are alcoholics, use drugs, and live lavish life-styles. We know about the housewife who begins "tipping" a little bit during the day due to boredom. She discovers, to her dismay, that she cannot start the day anymore without a drink. We have heard about the corporate executive who enjoys a "three martini lunch" and finds out too late that it has led to an excessive dependence on alcohol. Finally, we have heard about the successful middle manager who discovers that an increasing alcohol habit has turned into an increasing problem, and she has just lost her job, her good credit rating, and her family. She is baffled because she may not even drink on a daily basis. She wonders what happened to the days of wine and roses. Fortunately, it seems that these things usually happen to *other* people. No one wants to be saddled with a condition to which such social stigma is attached.

These naive stereotypes are extremely popular conceptions of alcoholics, and until recently they were almost exclusively the basis for the average American's understanding of alcoholism. Clearly, the most influential of these descriptions has historically been the skid row bum. However, enough people have been touched by an alcoholic in their personal lives that these other stereotypical situations have also become a part of the American folk system of defining and classifying alcoholics. We agree that if someone starts every morning with a drink and drinks all day, that person probably has an alcohol problem. We also will judge that someone is an "alcoholic" if that individual is drinking excessively and having problems getting to work or functioning properly when working. We condemn as "alcoholic" a man who gets drunk every day and beats his wife. If a successful man or woman has "lost everything" and is a hopeless drunk, then we can be fairly certain that he or she is an alcoholic. Unfortunately, we only know these things *after* the damage to the individual and those around the alcoholic has already been done. Rarely, do we recognize or reveal that it is happening in our own families and among our friends or coworkers until much too late in the process.

Scientific definition and classification of forms of drunkenness have not always been much better than these folk systems. There have been many attempts to classify alcoholics, define alcoholism, and suggest some solution to the problem. Most of the early attempts from the mid-nineteenth century to the mid-twentieth century were not very scientific. Generally, these early efforts were more interested in propagating a particular point of view in order to justify various disciplinary measures or punishments of drunkards. Babor and Lauerman (1986) provide an excellent review of these historical efforts at classification and clearly show that even today science has trouble defining the problem. It is not difficult to see how the average American may have trouble understanding alcoholism when one takes into account the significant differences of opinion within the scientific community. Many of these differences are due to the folk concepts of alcoholism that various researchers bring to scientific investigations (Tarter 1983) and that hamper efforts to define alcoholism.

DEFINITION OF ALCOHOLISM

One of the most problematic aspects of alcohol research has been the inability to describe alcoholism in such a way that everyone can agree and productively use the definition in the diagnosis, intervention, and treatment of various alcohol-related problems. Some researchers even go so far as to doubt the existence of any such entity as alcoholism; instead they maintain that variability in the numerous clusters of symptoms make up almost as many different "alcoholisms" as there are alcohol abusers (Pattison et al. 1977, Blane 1978). Other researchers or organizations, interested primarily in applications to social and political decisions, may have a tendency to define alcoholism socio-generically. This perspective tends to view any drinking behavior that may cause problems to the social system as indicative of alcoholism (Vaillant 1983). Such a definition, which is too broad, will include many individuals who are obviously not alcoholic and will often be considered absurd to the professional engaged in research (Davies 1976).

However, a number of researchers have attempted to define alcoholism in a productive manner. Vaillant (1983) identifies alcoholism as a continuum of negative consequences. Davies, working with Jellinek's (1960) definition states in his refinement that "alcoholism is intermittent or continual use of alcohol associated with dependency (psychological or physical) or harm in the sphere of mental, physical, or social activity" (Davies 1976: 69). Gallant offers a definition "based on patterns of impairment of functioning. A drinking problem which may require treatment exists if the use of alcohol continues despite significant interference in any one of the five major areas of a person's life" (1987: 2). Gallant identifies these major areas of life as (1) employment or studies, (2) marital, family, or living companion relationships, (3) interpersonal relationships, (4) legal problems, and (5) medical complications.

The National Institute on Alcohol Abuse and Alcoholism makes the distinction between alcohol abusers and alcohol dependent individuals (alcoholics). NIAAA characterizes the abuser as an individual who runs substantial risk of medical, psychological, social, and legal problems from single bouts of drinking or "the effects of persistent high-risk alcohol use." The alcoholic is characterized as an individual who definitely runs the same risks but also experiences "physical and psychological dependence on alcohol that results in impaired ability to control drinking behavior. This impairment in control represents the critical distinction between alcohol abuse and alcohol dependence" (NIAAA 1990: 2).

In almost all productive definitions of alcoholism, there are three particularly pertinent points: (1) the alcoholic is psychologically and/or physically dependent on the use of alcohol, (2) the alcoholic suffers harmful consequences from the use of alcohol, but continues to drink, and (3) the alcoholic suffers from impaired control over drinking behavior. There is also a fourth point that may be crucial to the definition of alcoholism—whether or not alcoholism is a disease.

THE DISEASE CONCEPT OF ALCOHOLISM

Historically, the disease concept of alcoholism has stood in sharp contrast to explanations that usually focused on the assumed morally degenerate nature of the alcoholic's character. Benjamin Rush, a physician and one of the men who signed the Declaration of Independence, wrote "An Inquiry into the Effects of Ardent Spirits upon the Human Body and Mind" in 1784. He accurately noted the chronic and intermittent symptoms associated with alcoholism, as well as aspects of the condition that appeared to be hereditary and those that seemed to be learned. He characterized the condition as a disease (Levine 1978). This disease concept has continued to compete with moralistic characterizations that maintain that chronic drunkenness is sinful and can only be corrected by the individual through an act of personal willpower (Marlatt et al. 1988).

A great deal of work by many different individuals and a diverse group of organizations has contributed significantly to the development of the disease concept of alcoholism (Babor and Lauerman 1986, Trice and Staudenmeier 1989). Jellinek (1960) is generally credited with the development of a disease model of alcoholism that was sufficiently rigorous to stimulate intensive scientific work based on the model, and many researchers have carefully investigated his various hypotheses and made necessary refinements to the disease concept of alcoholism. Much of the work in alcohol studies over the past 35 years has been specifically addressed to whether or not alcoholism can be considered a disease. Most of what we have discovered about alcoholism and other addictions has been the result of this particular focus in research.

Much of the speculation that alcoholism could be explained by biochemical disorders involving hypoglycemia, vitamin deficiencies, metabolic pathways, or an allergy to alcohol were quickly put to rest (Vaillant 1983). Nor, despite intensive efforts, has any single allele been discovered as an alcoholism gene. Numerous studies strongly support the hypothesis that some individuals are genetically predisposed to alcoholism (Goodwin 1983), but these studies can only account for a small proportion of alcoholism in the general population. Such evidence does not address many etiological questions regarding the disease concept of alcoholism (Vaillant 1983).

Clearly, a strictly medical model is not sufficient to explain the multivariate, behavioral manifestations of alcoholism. Furthermore, there are numerous examples that show "how our *beliefs* [italics added] about alcohol and alcohol consumers influence our assumptions about etiology" (Tarter 1983: 197). Most studies now recognize the "bio-psycho-social" complexity of alcoholism (Levin 1990), and although the disease concept that Jellinek described has been amended, it is still one of the most important considerations in any discussion of alcoholism. His ideas that alcoholism was characterized by a loss of control, and a progressive nature have been refined, but they are still regarded as essentially productive.

Bissell and Haberman note that it is extremely difficult to pinpoint "the onset of a disease that is typically, slowly progressive, episodic, shows marked diversity in the related signs or symptoms, and carries a high degree of social stigma" (1984: 13). In *Alcoholism in the Professions* they used certain bench marks in order to demonstrate the developing nature of alcoholism in the individual: (1) when they began to drink with regularity, (2) when drinking began to interfere with life, (3) when someone else first expressed concern about their drinking, and (4) when personal concerns began. These bench marks were also strongly suggested by the work of Woodruff and colleagues (1976), who found that a "yes" answer to any one of the three following questions could very accurately identify probable alcoholics: (1) Has your family ever objected to your drinking? (2) Did you ever think you drank too much in general? (3) Have others (such as friends, physicians, clergy) ever said, "You drink too much for your own good?"

These studies show that, although the etiology may vary, the symptoms may show a very high degree of diversity, and the patient may or may not respond to treatment, alcoholism appears to have some predictable effects on the life of the individual, to have a predictable subset of causes, to manifest itself in a variable, but definite progression of development, and to result in many serious consequences that require treatment.

TREATMENT OF ALCOHOLISM

Until recently, the treatment of alcoholism has had a vainglorious history. Many groups and individuals have attempted to relieve the suffering of the "hopeless alcoholic." In the nineteenth century, temperance and fraternal societies provided help based on the notion that drunkenness was a moral affliction and looked to a conversion experience to cure the alcoholic. During this time, many institutional organizations and asylums were established to study and treat habitual drunkenness, some of which advanced the idea of alcoholism as a disease. In addition to valid organizational approaches there were also various patent medicines and home remedies that touted different elixirs as cures. These almost invariably turned out to be potions of high alcoholic content, and therefore, strictly worthless in treating drunkenness (Levine 1984, Trice and Staudenmeier 1989).

In the early twentieth century, as psychoanalysis began to develop, many turned to psychotherapy to deal with alcoholism. However, as medical practitioners had found the "drunkard" to be especially hopeless regardless of the treatment regimen, so did the early psychotherapists. The lack of success in dealing with the problem of habitual drunkenness led many medical practitioners to confine themselves to the management of acute alcohol withdrawal, and they found themselves faced with the treatment of the same patients repeatedly. Some psychotherapists, such as Carl Jung, expressed the conviction that the chronic alcoholic was hopeless and that only a deep, transforming spiritual experience could help the alcoholic to recover (Kurtz 1979, Leach and Norris 1977, AA 1939).

Ironically, the period of national prohibition of alcohol ushered in with the passage of the Volstead Act by the U.S. Congress reduced the available support organizations that specialized in helping the alcoholic. The mistaken viewpoint that prohibition would solve the problem and the growing cultural values that fostered a greater acceptance of the use of alcohol during this period of time contributed to limited assistance for what many considered the "hopeless drunkard." Throughout the past 50 years, great efforts have been made in the scientific community to define the problem of alcoholism and develop effective treatment programs. Researchers and medical and psychological practitioners have made significant progress in the diagnosis, intervention, and treatment of alcoholism. Elaborate inpatient facilities for the management of acute alcohol withdrawal are widespread and available to a significant proportion of the population in the United States. Some of these facilities also provide extended inpatient care for those who may suffer from protracted withdrawal syndromes. There are also many outpatient facilities that provide these services to many individuals with less severe physical, neurological, or psychiatric problems.

Pharmacological treatment of alcoholism has become intense as physicians prescribe various drugs to manage withdrawal, ensure continued abstinence in alcohol dependent individuals (e.g., Antabuse), deal with underlying psychiatric pathologies, and reduce craving and consumption. While some of these agents have been shown to be effective in the short term, none seem to have demonstrated the ability to produce long-term success. They must be considered effective only as complimentary to other treatment strategies. This also seems to apply to most aversion therapies, only some of which are pharmacological (NIAAA 1990).

Many alcoholics may be genetically predisposed to alcoholism, and some alcoholics must cope with an acute, physical alcohol dependence that may respond to biochemical and medically based treatment alternatives. However, the most successful long-term management of the problem for the individual alcoholic has been achieved through various psychotherapeutic approaches. While some of these approaches are more likely than others to provide adequate treatment for the alcoholic, such individual therapies as psychotherapy and behavioral modification, such group therapies as family and marital therapy, and some socially therapeutic approaches that try to target the enhancement of communication, assertiveness, and resistance to peer pressure constitute the most favorable approach to long-term abstinence and sobriety.

The most controversial aspect of alcohol treatment research over the past 30 years may be whether or not abstinence should even be the long-term goal for the individual alcoholic. Many researchers have questioned the need for abstinence as a long-term goal and suggested that behavior modification could sufficiently enable alcoholics to learn to drink normally. Davies (1962) suggested that some alcohol dependent individuals could return to normal drinking in some cases. Later research initially supported this view. Sobell and Sobell (1973), working with state hospital inpatients in California, suggested that alcoholics could be trained to control their drinking. Armor and colleagues (1976) suggested that the ideal treatment goal of abstinence should be reconsidered, based on their study of individuals who had returned to drinking. Many professional and many lay people in the United States regarded such studies as proof that alcoholics could learn to drink normally and avoid the characteristic problems of alcohol dependence.

Other researchers have taken serious exception to the conclusion of these reports and the interpretation given to them by the authors and by the public. Vaillant concluded on the basis of a prospective study in which he followed over 600 subjects for over 40 years, that Davies's sample was extremely small and that

heart transplantation and lunar travel are of the greatest heuristic importance, but they are of little use to the millions who suffer from heart disease or an itch to visit the moon. Similarly, it is important for alcohol specialists to know that it is theoretically possible for alcohol dependent individuals to be taught to return to asymptomatic drinking; it is equally important for them to appreciate that abstinence may be a more practical and statistically more useful therapeutic focus. (Vaillant 1983: 235)

Sobell and Sobell's experimental project, in which they attempted to train alcoholic inpatients to drink normally, has been severely criticized on methodological grounds (Chalmers 1979) and in the interpretation of the data, which was severely hampered by inadequate long-term follow-up and study (Wallace 1983). Polich and colleagues (1980), in a four-year follow-up of the earlier study, revealed significant weaknesses in their initial approach and also supported Wallace's conclusion that "sustained non-problem drinking is not likely" (1981: 296). Although various researchers may still support the idea that alcoholics can return to drinking, it is "never a return to social or normal drinking, but only controlled or asymptomatic drinking" (Vaillant 1983: 218).

In recent years, many treatment programs have been proposed that suggest that abstinence should probably be the preferred treatment goal for those diagnosed as alcoholic. These studies and programs also recognize the essential importance of approaching the complex biological, psychological, social, and cultural problems of alcoholism from an interdisciplinary perspective. They stress the importance of early diagnosis, intervention, and individualized treatment regimens in response to the complex etiological and developmental nature of alcoholism. Most recognize a disease continuum, as it is manifest in alcoholics, and realize the necessity of extensive long-term aftercare, and social and personal support networks. Finally, many of these researchers and practitioners recognize the importance of Alcoholics Anonymous as a valuable treatment program in itself, or at the least, a very useful adjunct to psychotherapy when possible (Vaillant 1983, Bissell and Haberman 1984, Brown 1985, Levin 1987, Gallant 1987, Moos et al. 1990).

ALCOHOLICS ANONYMOUS

The mutual-help organization Alcoholics Anonymous (AA) was founded in Akron, Ohio in June, 1935 when a New York stockbroker named Bill Wilson sought out a surgeon named Robert Smith for a conversation about their common problem with alcohol. Bill W. and Dr. Bob, as they are often called in AA folklore, were both successful professionals—and alcoholics. Six months earlier, Wilson had been relieved of the compulsion to drink after having had an intense "spiritual" experience while undergoing withdrawal from alcohol. In Akron, on a business trip, he found himself tempted to have a drink in the bar of his hotel. He immediately began trying to find another alcoholic with which to share his experience in the hope that such "evangelism" would help him to not take a drink. He knew, from his own personal history, if he had even one drink, it would inevitably lead to a disastrous binge. This chance meeting proved to be the beginning of what would become the organization known as Alcoholics Anonymous.

The fellowship developed slowly at first. When *Alcoholics Anonymous*, which became commonly known as the Big Book, was initially published in 1939, the foreword began with the statement, "We of Alcoholics Anonymous, are more than one hundred men and women who have recovered from a seemingly hopeless state of mind and body. To show other alcoholics precisely how we have recovered is the main purpose of this book. . . . Many do not comprehend that the alcoholic is a very sick person. And besides we are sure that our way of living has its advantages for all"(AA 1976: xiii). From this limited beginning, AA has grown to be the single most influential organization in history that specializes in helping alcoholics recover from alcoholism. There are over 1 million alcoholic members in different groups in the United States and other parts of the world.

The impact of Alcoholics Anonymous has not been limited to only alcoholics. The 12-step program of AA is the primary plan of action that is suggested by the group to relieve the affliction of alcoholism. It has also been adapted to many other problems. Al Anon, which offers assistance to the families of alcoholics, Narcotics Anonymous and Synanon which offer help to drug addicts, Sex Addicts Anonymous, Overeaters Anonymous, Smokers Anonymous, and many other groups have adapted the 12-step program (*with the permission of Alcoholics Anonymous World Services, Inc.*) to assist individuals in overcoming a diverse set of problems that might be classified as addictive behaviors.

The history and development of AA has been well documented by researchers (Leach and Norris 1977, Kurtz 1979, Trice and Staudenmeier 1989) and also by the organization itself (AA 1939, AA 1957, AA 1967, AA 1980, AA 1984). Alcoholics Anonymous has generated intense discussion among members and among those in the scientific community as to the efficacy and relevance of its principles to the problem of alcoholism in general, and more specifically, to the individual alcoholic. This study intends to clarify the principles of Alcoholics Anonymous and address some of the questions and criticisms that have been voiced by those in the scientific community in order to better reveal and understand how and why Alcoholics Anonymous works. Through such an understanding, it may be possible to foster much greater cooperation among researchers and practitioners in medicine and psychology and the membership of AA. By gaining more thorough knowledge and understanding of why people drink, how drinking works as an adaptive mechanism, and how drinking becomes maladaptive and destructive for the alcoholic, we may be able to significantly relieve some of the terrible suffering that it causes in contemporary American society.

2
Culture and Consumption

Early anthropological observations concerning the use of alcohol were made in the context of general ethnography. None of the early investigators set out to focus on the use of alcohol as the primary subject of their research. However, given the widespread use of alcohol among different cultural groups around the world, it was readily apparent and frequently reported that the native production of alcoholic beverages was common (Marshall 1980). Most of this ethnographic work described small, traditional societies and sought to illuminate their ways of life. The role of ritual in understanding these comparatively different cultural realities played an extremely important part in ethnographic analysis and also in the development of anthropology as a discipline. Social organization and relations between groups and individuals were also considered to be of paramount importance to understanding the native conception of life within the society. Ritual and social life were the foci upon which much of anthropology grounded its most basic assumptions. As a result of this emphasis, early reports concerning alcoholic beverages tended to be in the context of ritual, ceremonial, and social uses.

In the early development of anthropological theory, the idea that every aspect of human behavior reflected the satisfaction of some basic human necessity was extremely important (Malinowski 1944). This view emphasized that all social institutions were the result of the drive to satisfy basic biological needs. In this way, all behaviors were thought to function for the essential good of individuals through the practical construction of the group and its distinct cultural reality. Subsequently, this early theory was amended to emphasize the primacy of social structures over biological drives to satisfy basic human needs (Radcliffe-Brown 1952). This counterproposal stressed that organized social institutions and structures developed and perpetuated themselves because they had drives of their own that were even stronger than the basic needs of the individuals within the group. Both of these perspectives were essentially viewed as functionalist. The use of alcohol was seen as another mechanism that established or maintained social and ritual relationships.

As with other aspects of culture, emphasis was on norms of the particular group under observation, and with very few exceptions very little attention was given to abnormal behavior in these early ethnographic studies.

In the 1940s two important anthropological reports focused on specific, critical questions regarding the use of alcohol. Ruth Bunzel (1940), working with Mayan Indian communities in Mexico and Guatemala, reported two very different systems of meaning that were integrated with the use of alcohol and drinking behavior. Her observations suggested that different patterns of drinking behavior could not be explained simply by the pharmacological effects of alcohol or the personality of the individual engaged in drinking. She concluded that the comparative cultural context of drinking was critical in order to account for crosscultural variation in drinking behavior. These comparative observations of two small communities indicated that learned behavior was essential to drunken comportment and suggested the need for more extensive crosscultural comparison in order to fully explain the meaning of drunkenness within any particular society. Donald Horton (1943) was the first to attempt such a broad-based comparison. Working with the Human Relations Area Files at Yale University he looked at 56 different cultural groups in order to test various psychocultural hypotheses statistically, particularly that alcohol use was related to the reduction of anxiety. He concluded that a direct relationship existed between drunkenness and the level of subsistence anxiety. He claimed to find more drunkenness in cultures where resources were less predictable. Even though this analysis was not subject to confirmation by direct observation, it stimulated an anthropological interest in why people drink.

Beginning in the 1950s many anthropologists started to address the comparative cultural context associated with alcohol use (Berreman 1956, Heath 1958, Mangin 1957, Sayres 1956, Simmons 1959). All these reports focused on specific patterns of drinking behavior and how the underlying significance varied. None of these articles appeared in the *American Anthropologist*. All these articles were published in *The Quarterly Journal of Studies on Alcohol*, which clearly demonstrates the miscellaneous quality of anthropological contributions to alcohol studies at that time. Anthropology had yet to focus direct attention on the study of alcohol use, but in the course of detailed descriptions many field workers recognized the importance of drinking patterns within the context of the sociocultural system (Heath 1987b). Drinking behaviors, by a functional perspective, were viewed as an integral aspect of establishing and maintaining social and ritual relations within and between cultures. These reports began to constitute a data base for crosscultural comparisons that demonstrated that drinking behavior varied substantially and that this diversity was the product of differences in the social, ceremonial, and ritual function of alcohol.

DEVELOPMENT OF THE ALCOHOL FOCUS IN ANTHROPOLOGY

These comparative observations prompted specific inquiries into patterns of alcohol use, and although there was little interest in alcoholism per se, many of these studies suggested hypotheses to explain why people might drink to achieve a state of drunkenness. Peter Field (1962) reanalyzed Horton's data and concluded that anxiety was not the best predictor of drunkenness. He found that the extent of drunkenness within a culture could be much better predicted by a lack of formalized corporate social structure. Bacon and colleagues (1965) suggested that the most accurate predictor within a particular culture was dependency-conflict theory. They hypothesized that childhood indulgence and a high cultural value on individual achievement in adulthood interacted in conflict and increased the likelihood of drunkenness. Klausner (1964) suggested the symbolic meaning and function of alcohol in any given society would be a fairly decent predictor of alcohol use and drunkenness. Somewhat later, McClelland and colleagues (1972) studied folktales of various groups and suggested that cultures that did not readily institutionalize "maleness" were more likely to foster heavy drinking. They hypothesized that men drink to feel more powerful.

These studies concerning crosscultural motivations and causes of drinking also led to questions about abnormal drinking behavior within a given cultural system. As anthropological investigations began to address abnormal as well as normative drunkenness, it became very apparent that not only was proper drinking behavior learned, but that abnormal behavior was also learned. The first extensive review to be published concerning the study of alcohol in anthropology showed that "cultural expectations define the ways in which drinking, both normal and abnormal, is done in a society" (Mandelbaum 1965: 288). Many comparisons of drinking patterns around the world revealed that drinking behavior, like all other behaviors in any given cultural system, were based on cultural expectations. Who drank and when and how much they drank was determined by custom. Drinking was prescribed in certain situations and prohibited in others. Sometimes the consumption of alcoholic beverages was considered sacred and at other times it was regarded as profane. Many anthropologists had regarded alcohol-consuming behavior as a part of the basic set of cultural rules. Examples of unusual behavior, such as Native Americans' abuse of alcohol, were considered aberrations.

MacAndrew and Edgerton (1969) challenged a great many of the basic accepted assumptions in the crosscultural investigation of drinking patterns. They suggested that drinking behaviors were governed by a slightly different set of rules and that the process of consuming alcoholic beverages was crossculturally governed by a "time out" in the normal expectations of behavior. When drinking, ordinary cultural expectations were suspended and temporarily replaced with a somewhat different set of guidelines for behavior. Using the crosscultural data base generated from earlier studies and ethnohistoric sources, they convincingly demonstrated that the grammar of drunken comportment was different than the everyday grammar used to control behavior. Abnormal behavior could also be viewed as learned within the context of this new assumption. This work put to rest the basic assumption that had first been questioned by Bunzel, that the pharmacological effects of alcohol on the individual personality would produce universal effects on behavior and supported the notion that even unusual behavior associated with the use of alcohol was based on rules that were acquired as members of the culture.

By the end of the 1960s the geographical scope of anthropological work regarding patterns of alcohol use was worldwide. The most basic thrust of this work clearly showed (1) that the drinking of alcoholic beverages and associated behavior was learned behavior, (2) that at least in all small-scale, traditional societies it was functional in the general cultural context, and (3) that seemingly deviant behaviors associated with drinking were also learned behaviors. Even though the consumption of alcoholic beverages had been of secondary interest in most research and much observation was still chiefly concerned with drinking patterns, anthropological work began to suggest that these data could be used to better understand health and social problems associated with alcohol dependence. The crosscultural comparison of drinking patterns began to take on more importance as anthropologists sought a more thorough understanding of these behaviors as an integral aspect of social explanation.

Throughout the next decade anthropologists began to focus on alcohol as it related to medical (Robbins 1977, Hippler 1974), psychological (Kearney 1970, Query and Query 1972, Robbins 1973), social (Rubington 1968, Ossenberg 1969, Kemnitzer 1972, Johnston 1973, Swartz and Romanucci-Ross 1974, Barnes 1977, Hill 1978), legal (Levy and Kunitz 1969, Jensen et al. 1977, Denzin 1977) economic (McLure and Thirsk 1978, Collman 1979), political (Hatch 1973), and applied (Albaugh and Anderson 1974, Manning 1977) questions in anthropology. Broader issues concerning alcohol use in these different contexts had become important, and some studies were conceived to specifically address such concerns. Although some of this work was directed to the study of alcohol issues in the United States, anthropologists directed most attention to the study of alcohol in relation to other cultures. Most of the work that was done in the context of American society generally focused on specific ethnic groups within the larger society, but there were some important exceptions.

Spradley's ethnography of urban, alcoholic nomads (1970) was an important work that used anthropological methods and analysis to detail the culture of skid row inhabitants and their interaction with the larger, social, political, and legal system in the country. It focused on the applied problem of public drunkenness as one aspect of alcoholism in America and had some important implications for policy decisions. Spradley and Mann (1975) detailed the specifics of bar culture in Brady's Bar. This work demonstrated that anthropological methods could be used to deal with unique cultural situations within the context of American society in order to better understand how the meaning of social behaviors associated with drinking varied in a complex society.

Everett and colleagues (1976) emphasized the interdisciplinary nature of alcohol studies. They brought together a collection of papers that demonstrated the vital importance of an anthropological perspective when addressing behaviors associated with alcohol use. By the end of the decade, Marshall (1979) had published the first general reader in the anthropological study of alcohol, which demonstrated that anthropologists had indeed achieved a worldwide perspective on alcohol issues. Furthermore, they had sufficient data and a critically different perspective that could have an important impact on the evergrowing field of alcohol studies. Some of these studies directly addressed etiologic and treatment issues concerning the role of culture on potential alcohol problems in complex societies (Westermeyer 1984, Cahalan 1969, Madsen 1974, Madsen 1979, Sadler 1977, Anderson 1979.)

Much of the anthropological work on alcohol use during this period had a greater impact on multidisciplinary studies of alcohol abuse and alcoholism than it did within the field of anthropology (Heath 1987b). This is particularly true of two very important investigations which focused on alcoholism and the efforts of the organization of Alcoholics Anonymous. Gregory Bateson (1971) proposed a theory of alcoholism in which he suggested that alcoholics are operating their lives on an epistemological error and that the spiritual program of Alcoholics Anonymous actually seeks to correct this error. This discussion concerning the "cybernetics of self" was very influential in alcohol studies, particularly among researchers in psychology, in its effort to explain alcoholism. Madsen's work with Alcoholics Anonymous (1974) was also very well received in alcohol studies and still has exceptional merit as intensive fieldwork with members of that organization. Madsen received substantial support from Bill Wilson, the co-founder of AA, and was able to observe at AA meetings, participate in outside activities, train some members as research assistants, and develop seminars with members in order to study various aspects of the nature-nurture controversy in alcohol research and therapy. Through this network he also followed some of those who had abandoned the practice of abstinence suggested by the AA program. Many AA members claim that some people with drinking problems may be referred to AA, but they may not be alcoholics even though someone else labeled them as such. Madsen suggests it is these people who can leave AA and successfully return to drinking. He also made some important observations about the futility of *real* alcoholics who attempt to return to normal drinking.

The development of an alcohol focus in anthropological research led to the development of a problem focus in the study of alcohol use by anthropologists. The focus on primarily social problems also more fully facilitated the integration of anthropological perspectives and methods into the general field of alcohol studies. Anthropologists are still significantly underrepresented in the field given the biological, social, cultural, and psychological complexity of alcoholism. A great deal of anthropological research is still chiefly concerned with functional drinking patterns in small, traditional cultures, but recent work in the study of alcohol is also represented by anthropologists interested in obtaining knowledge that can be applied to the problem of alcohol use within complex societies. Anthropologists have not simply followed the direction of other alcohol researchers in sociology, psychology, and biology; instead they have begun to apply the concepts of culture and adaptation in a holistic manner that is characteristic of anthropological inquiry and theory.

RECENT ANTHROPOLOGICAL CONTRIBUTIONS

Since 1980 there has been a relative explosion of work by anthropologists in the alcohol field. Naturally, since research on small societies is the traditional purview of anthropology, much work has continued to focus on patterns and meanings of drinking in exotic, small-scale societies. Such extensive crosscultural comparison has been key to understanding the meaning of alcohol use in various contexts (Heath 1984a, 1984b). However, anthropological contributions about problems associated with alcohol use in complex societies have increased dramatically. These efforts have not only made a significant impact on the interdisciplinary field of alcohol studies (Heath 1987a), but have also stimulated researchers from other disciplines to become more involved in anthropological forums and have facilitated a number of joint projects that offer a more holistic approach (Bennett 1984a).

The development of a focus on the problems associated with alcohol has also shifted the setting of much fieldwork from societies at lower levels of sociocultural integration to those at more complex levels of social organization. Heath (1983) presents a good summary of evidence that addiction, or the compulsive, often destructive need for habit-forming drugs, does not generally occur in traditional societies, except under conditions of social and cultural contact and change. It could be argued that "under conditions of social and cultural contact and change" would essentially include almost all cultural groups in the world at present. However, it is typical of anthropologists to approach the analysis of another group as if it still existed as a discrete and unique cultural system. Furthermore, there may be some heuristic value in such an approach to better understanding alcohol problems.

Room (1984), a sociologist and an experienced alcohol researcher, suggested that anthropologists have deflated the problems of alcohol in traditional societies because of a theoretical orientation that is functionalist and because most of these anthropologists have been enculturated as members of a post-prohibition culture that places high prestige on the use of alcoholic beverages. Most anthropologists concede that we are all affected by our own cultural baggage and that there have been theoretical and methodological shortcomings in past work, but they challenge the idea that the discipline has not produced a body of work that directly bears on the problems of alcohol (Bennett 1984b, Agar 1984, Heath 1984c, Leland 1984, Levy 1984, Madsen 1984, Marshall 1984). The Alcohol and Drug Study Group is an independent academic organization that has been affiliated with the American Anthropological Association since 1979. The very existence of this special group demonstrates that anthropology has developed a genuine focus on troublesome aspects of alcohol use and abuse.

Anthropological studies have focused on the alcohol problems encountered by minority ethnic groups within larger, complex societies and have included research regarding how and why such problems develop in these populations and what treatment alternatives might be appropriate and effective. Heath and colleagues (1981a) and Douglas (1987) provide an excellent view of theoretical and methodological considerations. Many of these studies show that even though much of the problem focus concerns smaller cultural groups within larger societies, anthropology is in the process of addressing questions that are of an applied interest to American society. A forum in the *Journal of Studies in Alcohol* that includes work by Strug (1981), Cohen and colleagues (1981), Rodin (1981), Strug and Hyman (1981), and Waddell (1981) represents an important anthropological concentration on issues that directly concern alcohol problems in the United States.

The cultural ecology of alcohol use as an adaptive mechanism in the context of acculturation and how it may become maladaptive at times has received important consideration (Gordon 1984, Hill 1984). Work has been addressed to the interaction of cultural factors with treatment goals (Levinson 1983) and methodological questions have been raised regarding anthropological work in various treatment settings (Waddell 1984). Perhaps most important, investigation into the role of the family in alcoholism has clearly indicated that observational methods characteristic of anthropology are an excellent means of gathering qualitative data that provide the proper long-term perspective that is needed to study alcoholism (Ablon 1984). According to Wallace (1983), it is precisely such long-term observation in anthropological perspective that has been lacking in the interdisciplinary study of alcoholism in the United States.

GOALS OF THE STUDY

There is a definite need for a more active anthropological research perspective in the alcohol field. Clearly, alcoholism is a problem that begs to be studied in a holistic sense. The discipline of anthropology has always regarded itself as uniquely qualified to approach any aspect of human behavior as a product of biological, psychological, social, and cultural forces. The complex bio-psycho-social nature of alcoholism makes it the perfect problem for anthropologists. Not only are the various theories of human behavior that have been developed in anthropology fundamentally suited to address the problem of alcoholism in modern American society, but specific ethnographic field methods of participation and observation can reveal important data that are not accessible through the more quantitative measures preferred by many epidemiologists, psychologists, and sociologists. This is especially accurate in studies of treatment settings in general, and Alcoholics Anonymous in particular. Although there has been a great deal of work published regarding Alcoholics Anonymous, much of it is misinformed. Anonymity among members of the organization functions to restrict access to the type of quantitative data researchers often believe is necessary. Researchers have often encountered resistance in their attempts to observe the process of recovery within AA. Even when allowed to attend meetings as observers, their very presence alters the event. There is also much doubt as to what extent members are frank, honest, and open in response to interview procedures with outsiders.

Alcoholics Anonymous has been characterized as a self-help organization, a cult, a crisis cult, a voluntary association, and a folk cure. In reality, it is the single most successful program of treatment for alcoholism over the past 60 years. Despite prodigious efforts to learn how and why it is effective, there exists no adequate ethnographic description of this community of recovering alcoholics. The primary goal of this research is to provide such a description of this community in order to understand the basic process of alcoholism, including development, practice, and recovery in urban American culture. Equipped with a better understanding, we may be able to develop a foundation for further anthropological study of alcoholism, Alcoholics Anonymous, and other potential treatment programs in the United States and cross-culturally. The primary hope of this study is a better understanding in the specific context of culture and adaptation, which are of critical importance to anthropological theory.

METHOD OF INVESTIGATION

The primary means of investigation in this study consisted of participation and observation. While there have been many studies concerning recovery, some of which have dealt with the program of Alcoholics Anonymous, there is no other work that deals with this particular program of recovery from the point of view of the recovering alcoholic. Incredible resources have been invested in the study of the effects of alcohol on the body and the mind, as well as the number of accidents and injuries that result from the common use of alcohol. Many studies have utilized only limited participation and observation to collect information concerning the recovery process. However, there has been no specific anthropological study characterized by sufficiently intensive participation and observation over an adequately long period of time to fully understand the recovery process. This study is an attempt to describe the program of Alcoholics Anonymous from the view of individuals who are living, acting, thinking participants in the process.

Early anthropologists made extensive studies in which they attempted to live the cultural reality of a different society. At the beginning of such a period of fieldwork they knew little or nothing about the societies they were trying to study, not even the language. They began by learning the language, and as they began to understand how the people expressed themselves they were able to begin to understand how they conceived of themselves in relation to rest of their world. This is the approach I have taken in this study. I started with only a minimal understanding of Alcoholics Anonymous. I began to learn the language, what was meant by various words and phrases, and developed concepts as a result of learning such expressions. Once I could operationalize these concepts in daily life, through my attitudes and actions, I began to live fully as a participant in this distinctive group within American culture. Through this work I began to fully appreciate the subjective experience of the recovering alcoholic, and I developed a perspective on alcoholism, recovery, relapse, and the world view of someone engaged in the program, that would not have even been possible through interviews or other constructs that attempt to characterize the exact demographic and personality factors that might constitute the group "alcoholics." Nor would have attendance, as an outsider, at 30 or 40 "open" meetings of AA facilitated such an understanding. I was able to function within the group as an accepted participant in Alcoholics Anonymous. Through this approach I obtained information generally inaccessible to researchers.

The information I was able to obtain through this method of investigation provided me with a unique opportunity to understand what people bring to the program of Alcoholics Anonymous from their experience as members of American society, their cultural expectations, their ideas about their place in the world around them, and their expectations of life. I was able to see directly how language and culture initiate and perpetuate the belief system of the actively practicing alcoholic and how language and culture also effect change in that system of belief as the recovering alcoholic lives the program of Alcoholics Anonymous. From March 1992 through August 1995 I attended more than 600 meetings of Alcoholics Anonymous. I attended open, closed, speaker, discussion, and group conscience meetings. I engaged in at least as many hours of conversation with a variety of members. I went to social gatherings and developed a set of social acquaintances. Although I visited many different AA groups within the Dallas area, my experience was intensively based in one small group. I became a member of AA in an attempt to deal with my own alcohol problem. The problem began almost immediately upon my beginning to use alcohol and, as is the case with many other alcoholics, became progressively worse over the years.

The first time I attended AA meetings was at the behest of the Dallas County Adult Probation Department as a requirement of probationary status due to a DWI (driving while intoxicated), charge in February of 1987. I realized at the time that I was having problems with alcohol. I scored extremely high on diagnostic tests given to determine whether or not an individual might be alcoholic, but I still had grave reservations about the necessity of attending AA meetings. When it was suggested that attendance at two meetings a week be required, my strong protests that there was no time available to attend so many meetings persuaded the man in charge of the evaluation to accept this lame excuse and agreed that one meeting a week would be satisfactory. I attended regular Sunday morning speaker meetings once every week for the two years of my probation. Although I did not keep records of these visits at the time, I probably missed no more than 10 of these weekly meetings over the course of the probation. I found the meetings to be humiliating and felt that my situation was very different from the vast majority of those in attendance, yet I was willing to attend the meetings because my behavior with regard to alcohol had disturbed me. I had committed various insults and offenses against others (my family and friends in particular) and felt that I needed some exposure to people who openly admitted they were alcoholic. It was very difficult to admit that I was an alcoholic, but I did so with the feeling that admitting that I had a problem would definitely make a big difference in drinking behavior. After a predictable 14-month judicial delay, I went to my very first AA meeting in April of 1988. It was a typical experience of first contact with Alcoholics Anonymous.

As I entered the meeting place, I observed the other people sitting around waiting for the meeting to begin. There were only six to eight people in the room when I entered. At least half of them extended cordial greetings and two of them introduced themselves. A strong feeling of guilt and embarrassment was present. I felt they thought I was there to surrender, turn myself in to the alcohol authorities. This is very common for most alcoholics at the first AA meeting. The primary motivation for going to AA was to satisfy the requirements of probation, yet I believed there was a problem with alcohol in my life and felt the exposure might change my drinking behavior. When I walked through the door, I had no intention of accepting "total abstinence" as a solution. After listening to the speaker for an hour that morning, I had heard enough similarity between the story he told and my own experience to accept a desire chip, a small metal token symbolizing the desire to quit drinking. Extremely inspired by the possibilities of abstinence, I was able to not take a drink for about a week.

Although I had been truly inspired, I was not convinced that total abstinence was necessary in my case. The more I listened to these AA stories, the more striking were the qualitative and quantitative differences between these people and myself. I made a conscious decision that I probably was not an alcoholic, or at the very worst, a small alcoholic compared to the severe, massive self-descriptions of these people who were obviously out of control. I confirmed that what I needed was to change my drinking habits. I had already changed my beverage of preference before going to the first AA meeting in an effort to change my behavior. Abstinence from hard liquor and listening to a weekly horror story at speaker meetings, combined with an intense effort to control my intake of alcohol, basically mitigated against any devastating experiences, but it did not eliminate them. It only decreased the frequency. After I completed probation, I quit attending AA meetings. For the next two years I continued to use alcohol excessively, went back to drinking whatever I preferred—especially distilled spirits—and essentially stopped trying to monitor the amount. I just let go and quit worrying about controlling the drinking and "enjoyed" myself.

During that first period of AA attendance, one of the primary differences I perceived between myself and the others was that most talked of drinking every day and of the devastating compulsion to drink every day.They talked about how they would swear over and over that they would not drink anymore and even though they were entirely sincere in the morning, by evening they could not keep themselves from drinking. I had never drunk every day. I had never had the compulsion to drink every day. I only drank a couple of times each week, usually on the weekends. I didn't feel that the label of alcoholic fit my situation. They also talked about how they were compelled to take a drink in the morning in order to deal with the "shakes." My hangovers were often quite severe, but never had I taken a drink to deal with feeling bad the next morning. That was the kind of thing that alcoholics did. I didn't drink in the morning, so I wasn't an alcoholic, I rationalized. They talked about losing their jobs because of their drunkenness. At the time, I was employed and didn't feel that I had ever lost a job due to my use of alcohol, so I couldn't be an alcoholic. I felt that I was a person who just had problems with the *amount* of alcohol I consumed. Everything I heard, I rationalized. I decided I wasn't an alcoholic, although I conceded I was "a problem drinker." There were too many differences between my situation and the stories they told for me to accept the label or any kinship.

Although many of these alcoholics expressed the opinion that my condition simply had not progressed to the point they were talking about, I essentially resisted the suggestion that alcoholism was "progressive" and that I would "get to that point eventually" if I continued to drink. I rejected this application of what I considered the AA myth to my personal situation. When I later entered the program of AA as a volunteer, my condition showed significant progression. I was having almost no success in resisting the urge to drink daily. Sometimes I took a drink in the morning. On a regular basis, I missed work due to hangovers, I had not been considered for promotions, and I had lost jobs as a direct result of my alcohol use. Everything they predicted had occurred. I accepted the fact that I was an alcoholic.

GOING BACK TO AA

I awoke in the most depressed state I can ever recall. I dressed and went to work, but all day could only think about what I had to do after work. I was going to go to an AA meeting. At six o'clock I left work and went to a different group than the one I had attended before. I arrived as the earlier meeting was breaking up. As I walked through the door, I almost turned and walked back out, but I forced myself to take a step down the long, 120-foot corridor. I was looking down a narrow hallway at the end of which I could see a couple of big coffee urns, some signs on the wall, and some people.

I began to walk toward the people and the sounds of conversation became audible. About halfway, some people came out of the doorway on the right and looked at me. The way they looked seemed to say that they knew why I was there. They knew about this last DWI, they knew I had rolled that subaru down that mountain eight years ago, they knew that on countless occassions I had violently erupted and harmed someone I cared about. They knew I was working in the car business and couldn't sell a car if I wanted to. They knew that I was broke, that I owed my parents and everybody else money, that I was alcoholic, that I couldn't keep living this way, that there was no reason to, and that I had so completely devastated my own image of myself that I wanted to die to be relieved of the embarrassment of my life. They knew that I was finally coming to an AA meeting to turn myself in.

I dragged myself up to the coffee urns and the room opened into a 65 by 25 foot space. Another room was on the far side enclosed in glass. I got some coffee and turned to see a man setting up some tables in preparation for the next meeting. I set the coffee down and began to help him set up the chairs. He greeted me, spoke in a friendly manner, and described the basic set up of the chairs, how far apart the rows should be, an so on. As long as I acted, I didn't feel such an intense fear of being out of place. When that was finished, I emptied a number of ashtrays and sat down. There were only 10 or 12 people present, some of them were talking to one another, others getting coffee, some standing, and a couple sitting. As I watched others come in, sit down, and greet one another, I noticed they acted happy. Many of them seemed to be in very good spirits and were quite well dressed. I felt that I had been right in choosing this group because they seemed to be people of a somewhat higher, socio-economic class than the members of the last AA group I had quit visiting two years before. Perhaps I could relate to these people a little better. A podium stood at the left front of the meeting hall and around the room hung various signs and plaques. The first one that caught my attention hung at the front and read, "EXPECT A MIRACLE." At that moment I knew that I needed a miracle, but I didn't expect one. My life, any kind of meaningful existence, had eluded me. Life had become totally meaningless and the enthusiasm of life before alcohol had vanished. If I couldn't quit drinking, I might as well shoot myself, now.

In the meeting hall, other things hung on the wall. The Twelve Steps were prominently displayed. I read the first one, "We admitted that we were powerless over alcohol and that our lives had become unmanageable." I wasn't having any trouble with that one. "Came to believe that only a power greater than ourselves could restore us to sanity," read the second. I felt insane, and I wished there was a God. The other steps provoked a lot of questions. This is what I have to do? How? How do you do that? How can this possibly work? One sign was titled "On the Beam" and listed the positive characteristics of "Faith, Hope, Generosity, Charity, Aspiration, Patience, Sympathy, Non Interference, Kindness, Courage, Forgiveness, Duty, and Love." I thought, this is going to be tough to take. Another sign was titled "Off the Beam" and listed the negative characteristics of "Fear, Worry, Anger, Jealousy, Criticism, Vanity, Hatred, Envy, Hypocrisy, Prejudice, Selfishness, and Greed." I thought, now there is something that I can relate to. I had no idea how this could possibly work.

The chair of the meeting led the introduction and someone read "How It Works" from the Big Book of Alcoholics Anonymous, and a man told "his story" for 45 or 50 minutes. His story was one about a middle-aged, but youthful and successful professional. Through the course of his many years of alcohol use he had become alcoholic and watched his personal and professional success slip progressively further from him. It was not the story of some skid row bum, but someone who had all the advantages this society has to offer in terms of education and opportunity and still managed to become an alcoholic. More important, he was at an AA meeting telling a story, the moral of which stated that life could be different if he didn't take that first drink. At the end of the meeting, I went up and got a desire chip, but I was bewildered and not very optimistic. The thundering applause was embarrassing. After the meeting one "old-timer" approached, offered congratulations, and asked if I needed some phone numbers. I did, he provided his, and said not to hesitate to call. A few others offered congratulations and said, "Come back." I left and went home.

The first few days and weeks were characterized by two overwhelming feelings. First, the feeling that there was hope. I went to meetings and saw people who were destroying their lives with alcohol before, but who now were happier and leading productive lives. But despair was the other feeling. I still couldn't see how I could make it the rest of my life without drinking. The thought kept me more in the state of hopelessness, than in hope, but I truly felt my life depended on changing, so I tried. I didn't drink after work; instead I went to meetings. In that way I began replacing the habit of drinking with another social activity, but I was still in despair.

It was the decision to return to the original AA club I had attended that changed my sense of despair to one of cautious hope. I was getting off late from work on the first Saturday night of my AA attendance. I had been sober a week. There wasn't a meeting after eight o'clock at the group I had been attending, so I looked up the phone number of the other club, called and confirmed that the memory I had of a "candlelight" meeting at 10:00 P.M. over there was real. I had gone to that club for two years during the period of probation I had received for the last DWI. I had only gone on Sundays, to "speaker meetings" such as I attended the first week. I didn't want to go to a discussion meeting and give myself away, but I felt that if I didn't go to participate in the AA process, I might give in to the nagging urge that I had been having to drink that evening. I arrived at the club early and drank coffee in silence as others milled around. They finally lit the candles, turned off the lights, and began the discussion. As the others related their tales in the dimly lit room, I began to be overwhelmed by the certainty that I had to participate in my own recovery. Comforted somewhat by the darkness of the room and by this belief, I spoke up when I was called on. I started talking in the most general terms about the necessity of quitting drinking. Fortunately, the man who was next to speak said he had been in the AA program for nine years and had remained sober, but that he "still hadn't quit drinking." He went on to explain that it was only by concentrating on "one day at a time" that he had been able to not drink for nine years. *This* was the first flash of insight. During that first week I had not had a drink and had gone to an AA meeting every day, but I had not participated in any way except to get myself to the meetings. This first participation yielded results. The idea of "one day at a time" restored my hope. With success measured by the day, I could see some usefulness in the program. If success were only to be measured in the following *years* of sobriety, I could not have any confidence in the utility of this approach. At the club, participation in the discussions became more comfortable. Many people with some length of sobriety took an interest and tried to be of help by staying after the meetings to talk or by just saying, "Come back." I became a member of the group as "*their* meetings" slowly became "*our* meetings." After I had accepted the program of AA as the best hope for recovery, many good things began to happen. My attitudes toward many things began to change, and I became open to many ideas that I had previously rejected.

Basically, this fieldwork did not begin with attendance at meetings of AA in 1988 or 1992, but began in the fall of 1978, my first semester of graduate school. Until that point in life, I had never used alcohol. Invited repeatedly for a little innocent fellowship at "happy hour" on Friday afternoon with some of the other graduate students, I began to seriously enjoy alcohol intoxication and drinking large amounts of alcohol. I became the star of the show, and a couple of graduate school cohorts started calling me "Wild Man." I liked that, but I began to have problems almost immediately and occasionally people suggested that perhaps I shouldn't drink so much. For the next thirteen and a half years, I progressively used alcohol until I had become a solid, practicing alcoholic. I was a periodic and binge drinker, but an alcoholic nonetheless. This may seem unfortunate, but it actually provided a foundation to fully appreciate why some alcoholics seek help through the program of AA, even when they have rejected the idea previously. It also gave me a good opportunity to understand what they bring with them to the AA program and the essential openness necessary to recover from alcoholism. Through real participation and membership in the group, I gathered information from others in the program that was offered from their experience. I was able to see positive and negative aspects of participation in AA as it relates to an individual's recovery.

RETURN TO RESEARCH

When I first went back to AA, a member told me, "Just hang in there. If you can just stay sober for a while, your perspective on everything will begin to change." He was right. After approximately three months of not drinking, it occurred to me that Alcoholics Anonymous was a distinctive community within American culture. It was obvious that they shared a unique worldview that contrasted to many popular American values, attitudes, and beliefs, and that they were engaged in a group psychotherapeutic exercise that used language as the primary tool to foster a radical change in the behavior of the alcoholic. For many, it worked. Fascinated, I decided to make an anthropological study of the process of recovery. A search of the literature in the field revealed a great deal of interdisciplinary work, mostly in psychology, sociology, theology, education, communications, and rhetoric, but almost no in-depth work in anthropology that focused specifically on Alcoholics Anonymous. There was no adequate ethnographic description of the organization or the people. I believed this was a significant oversight and embarked on this project in the firm hope that an anthropological perspective could offer great insight into the nature of the development of alcoholism, the practice of alcoholism, and the recovery from alcoholism.

Given the value with which members of AA hold the concept of anonymity, the first thing was to explore the possibility of this research with members of the group. I confided to a few of the members that I was going to write a book about AA and was met with extreme ambivalence. Some said that I should just work the steps and not worry about the book. Some seemed to feel that I was engaged in some type of denial about alcoholism. As one said, "Everything that needs to be in a book is in the Big Book." Most of the people I told about my plans for turning the experience into a research project thought it was a good idea and an indication that I was recovering. But, even though I had divulged a great deal of personal information about myself and my life to other members of the group, I did not stand and make an announcement in order to make it generally known that I was engaged in research. For one thing, if I told a number of people in the group, then they told the others. The principle of anonymity has its practical limits. I felt that to present this research in a high-profile manner would have changed their approach and attitude toward me, which was as of a fellow member of AA. They might begin to consider me a researcher and someone to be viewed with suspicion, rather than as a viable member of the group seeking assistance with alcohol dependency. For the same reasons, I decided early on to forego any attempt at formal, structured interviews or to gather demographic data that would have surely caused some to feel their anonymity might be in jeopardy. I also refrained from identifying anyone except on the most general basis of approximate age, sex, and length of sobriety.

There is a common anti-intellectualism among many members of AA regarding scientific studies of alcoholism. I found this bias alive and well in my discussions with AA members. They often expressed that there was no scientific understanding of the problem that could be of much use to the recovering alcoholic. Many individuals in AA have had ample experience with the health care system, which was not effective in dealing with their alcoholism. Given this fact, such bias is understandable. I started to worry about my own bias as work began in earnest. I wanted to distance myself from other members in an attempt to be objective. I succeeded in achieving enough distance to bring on a relapse and then realized that I could not do this project from a totally detached perspective. The only way I could accomplish the study was as a sober, living participant in this reality. However, I did realize that even though I could not be strictly objective, this is hardly the ideal in very much ethnographic work anyway (Geertz 1988). In fact, participant observation in Alcoholics Anonymous can *only* be achieved by a member.

Tedlock (1991) carefully details much ethnographic work as an observation of participation. The ethnographer cannot be expected to be actively engaged in the reality of the people studied and still remain a dispassionate, objective observer. She also maintains that the production of the written report cannot eliminate the self, but that self and other must be "presented together within a single narrative ethnography, focused on the character and process of the ethnographic dialogue" (1991: 69). Obviously, this study must be an observation of participation and this report must be an ethnographic narrative. Narayan argues very convincingly "for a reorientation in the ways that we perceive anthropologists as 'outside' or 'inside' a society." She maintains that all anthropologists are engaged in a process of shifting identities and that the ethnographic encounter is essentially a subjective one. Native anthropologists are not always necessarily "insiders" because "the very nature of researching what to others is taken-for-granted reality creates an uneasy distance." She concludes that "by situating ourselves as subjects simultaneously touched by life-experience and swayed by professional concerns, we can acknowledge the hybrid and positioned nature of our identities" (1993: 682). Finally, another anthropologist points out that even though we are engaged in the "dissolution and reconstitution of self" as a by-product of ethnographic investigation, we need not despair of never being able to really know anything. "Rather, such grounding in context should endow us with humility and draw our attention to the embeddedness of our understanding in human relationships and human finitude" (Kondo 1986: 86). As we shall see, these observations concerning the self and other are not only important in the method of this study, but have an important theoretical bearing on the process of alcoholism as well.

Culture has been defined in many ways over the course of the twentieth century, but it can best be described as any shared system of beliefs, behaviors, and energetic exchanges that are dependent upon the use of symbols. When studying many small, traditional societies, it is relatively apparent that such systems are shared between most or all of the members. In order to study American culture, we can examine the larger society in terms of beliefs or behaviors that are shared by all, but essentially we must look at many different variations or subsystems that are shared by specific, but limited groups. Even though such subgroups may exhibit beliefs and behaviors that are not shared by many others outside that particular group, they do share many things in common, and are parts of the whole that lend themselves well to investigation (Spindler and Spindler 1983). This study was based on the experience of recovering alcoholics in Alcoholics Anonymous and relied on individuals' reports concerning the development of alcoholism. They provided information about enculturation into American society and the drinking culture, about the personal nature of alcohol dependence, and about the process of recovery. Although there is good reason to expect some problems with regard to informant accuracy, especially with respect to the recollection of health-seeking behavior, communication, and social interaction, this should not and cannot preclude the use of such information. An individual's memory may vary, particularly when dealing with altered states of consciousness, but we must recognize this limitation and proceed in an effort to validate such retrospective data (Bernard et al. 1984). Furthermore, the "drinker's story" has been clearly identified as important and often overlooked in the context of alcohol studies (Topper 1981).

The accuracy of specific assertions made by individuals concerning past history could not be verified objectively, but most subjects of this study reported a shared experience in the development of alcohol dependence and in their recovery through the program of Alcoholics Anonymous. Most of the data reported in this study came from members who had achieved significant periods of sobriety. All asserted that their recollection of past events was much more reliable after becoming sober than it had been during their drinking careers, or even during the achievement of early sobriety (Brown 1985). Observations made during the course of this study reflect intensive interaction with approximately 60 individuals sustained over the course of three years. A slightly greater proportion of men were observed. Most of the subjects were between 35 and 55 years of age. People in their 40s seem to be heavily represented in AA. In addition to such prolonged participation involving individuals at the same AA club, observations were also made at a dozen other groups in the metropolitan area. These observations involved 300 to 500 additional individuals and effectively validated the information gathered from members at the club concerning their common experience. This is precisely the type of long-term, observational study that has been needed in order to better understand the dynamics of recovery in AA (Wallace 1983).

Most of the observations during this study were made at meetings of Alcoholics Anonymous. While I attended speaker meetings, most of the real observation of participation was made at discussion meetings. Due to the basic structure of the AA discussion meeting and the small, intimate environment of the group in which most of the observations were made, I was able to use these gatherings as a focus group. Although focus groups are not particularly well suited to objective measures, they are extremely helpful in discovering the intensity of a issue (Bernard 1988). I was able to repeatedly observe such discussions of issues and at times was able to chair a meeting or otherwise redirect attention to specific issues that I thought still needed to be examined in the context of this study.

The focus on drinkers' stories and the specific language with which they describe their attitudes, values, and beliefs clearly demonstrate that members of Alcoholics Anonymous constitute a distinctive cultural entity. They share a common viewpoint of their relationship to the rest of the world and they interact in the context of a specific speech community. It is interesting to note that this speech community cannot be identified through phonological or syntactic peculiarities that distinguish it from Standard American English, as is usually the case with other many speech communities that have been the subject of study in the United States. Instead, it is characterized by a unique semantic structure.

Members of Alcoholics Anonymous in the United Stated come from a diverse demographic, social, psychological, and linguistic set of populations. However, they share not only the common experience of alcoholism and related behavioral problems, but a distinctive referential system of meaning in recovery. When AA members refer to such concepts as surrender, acceptance, pride, powerlessness, control, resentments, a higher power, or God, these terms may have a much different meaning to members of the AA culture than they generally convey to other members of American society. While there is some overlap and similarity with the larger society, the referential system is basically foreign to most people outside of AA. It is through the acquisition of this new language that Alcoholics Anonymous enculturates new members into the group and perpetuates itself as a viable and unique cultural community within American society (Marrus 1988).

All the observations, quotations, attitudes, beliefs, values, insights, objections, hopes, fears, defeats, and conquests that I describe in the next four chapters are the result of my participation in American culture, my life experience as a "practicing" alcoholic for over 13 years, my observations and reactions as a casual, mandated observer of Alcoholics Anonymous for 2 years, my participation as an active member of AA for over 3 years, and my adult life as a student and teacher of anthropology for the past 25 years. I was there. Most of what I have written about Alcoholics Anonymous I heard in a meeting, usually repeatedly. Many individual members in AA have been instrumental in communicating the goals and action of the program of AA, and without their insight, experience, strength, and hope, I would know none of what follows regarding alcoholism. I would not even be sober and able to write this report.

3

Qualifications, Referrals, and Affiliation

Speakers at meetings often begin their stories by expressing the need to "qualify" themselves as alcoholics. It is also common for individuals to make reference to their "qualifications" as they participate in discussions. These statements usually consist of information concerning life history, attitudes and beliefs concerning self and others, development of alcohol use, loss of control, and the denial of an alcohol problem in the context of "how I got to Alcoholics Anonymous."

Researchers have attempted to identify AA members on the basis of specific personality and demographic characteristics. Some have suggested that individuals are more likely to affiliate with AA if they are authoritarian and conformist, characterized by greater affiliative and group dependency needs, more prone to guilt concerning their past behavior, extremely religious, relatively simple in their cognitive processes, and field dependent in their perceptual systems (Ogborne and Glaser 1981, O'Leary et al. 1980, Bean 1975, and Leach 1973). However, these qualities are, in some measure, encouraged by participation in the program of AA. It is far more likely that many of these traits are *acquired as a result of affiliation* and should be expected in any sample of regular membership. Such variables as, "race, religion, education, socioeconomic status, employment status, legal status, parental socioeconomic status, adult social competence, cognitive functioning, and type of religion appear unrelated to membership in AA" (Emrick 1989b: 38). Furthermore, "efforts to isolate the 'AA personality' are apparently proving to be as unfruitful as were earlier attempts to define an alcoholic personality" (Emrick 1989b: 41).

Variation among individuals in AA is extensive. Active members come from all socio-economic and ethnic groups (Baekland et al. 1975, Bissell and Haberman 1984) and exhibit many different cognitive styles and personality characteristics. While AA members may or may not be representative of the total population of alcoholics (Emrick et al. 1977), it has not been possible to predict, on the basis of unique demographic or personality characteristics, which individuals will be most likely to affiliate with and benefit from AA (Edwards 1982). However, based on information obtained from subjects in this study, there are certain behavioral and experiential characteristics that virtually all active AA members share to some extent. Members claim that legal problems, poor family relationships, social isolation, employment and financial difficulties, health concerns, and serious emotional disturbances led them to accept the program of AA as a possible solution. Loss of control over their drinking was significantly symptomatic and led to the loss of control over their daily lives (Brown 1985, Levin 1987). Denial of an alcohol problem, or more specifically, denial of alcoholism is also characteristic. As members often stated, "I continued doing the same thing expecting different results," which compounded the difficulties that led them to AA.

COURT ORDERED INTERVENTION

Introduction to Alcoholics Anonymous through court ordered intervention is common. The legal system, heavily burdened with drunk drivers, often refers offenders to AA in an attempt to help individuals who may have an alcohol problem. Studies of court ordered participation have indicated that AA is not particularly effective and sometimes markedly less effective than other treatments in dealing with this particular group (Ditman et al. 1967, Brandsma et al. 1980), but there is significant, active participation in AA membership among those referred by the criminal justice system.

Most members introduced to AA through this type of legal coercion did not respond immediately in a positive way. They went to meetings because they were required to attend. One member reflected on the resentments that many others also claim to have developed when forced to attend AA "I couldn't believe I had to sit around and listen to a bunch of alcoholics complain about the fact they couldn't handle their alcohol." Another member said at one time he was given the choice of 6 months in jail or 90 AA meetings in 90 days. He went to one meeting and went back to the judge and said, "I'll take the 6 months. I can't handle them AA meetings." Virtually all members initially referred to AA by the legal system responded exactly as predicted in the studies cited above. They were angry to be identified with a "bunch of alcoholics." They considered themselves qualitatively different from the others they observed in the program. Many felt the only problem they had, as one member put it, "was with the police. If they'd just quit stopping me, everything would be fine."

Most would admit no problem with alcohol and rarely did they think they were alcoholic. They listened to the stories in the meetings and rationalized any similarities. These individuals almost always continued to drink or returned to drinking after a brief period of abstinence. They simply could not accept the label of alcoholic. Some of them finally came to accept the necessity of trying to work the program because of the threat of incarceration as a result of additional, sometimes felony, DWI charges. However, even faced with such threats to personal freedom, many of these individuals began attending without accepting the identity of an alcoholic. For these individuals, such acceptance came slowly and grudgingly, only after intensive exposure to the principles, attitudes, and beliefs expressed through the specialized language of Alcoholics Anonymous.

Since almost all of these court appointed individuals testify to the inability to accept the alcoholic label, since virtually all of them claim they violently rejected AA initially, and since many of them are still in evidence years later as active, participating members of AA, it is obvious there is some justification for requiring all DWI offenders to attend some AA meetings. Individuals who are truly not alcoholic will probably be able to respond to the embarrassment, expense, and hassle by changing drinking behaviors that are destructive or dangerous. Most members admit that when they finally came to the end and they were "ready to give up," at the very least, the initial court mandated exposure to the program assured them of having useful information regarding the possibility of assistance through the AA program.

FAMILY AND SOCIAL PROBLEMS

Alcoholism is not an affliction that limits itself to the destruction of the individual alcoholic, but usually manifests itself as a family disorder as well (Ablon 1984, Vaillant 1983, Moos et al. 1990, Brown 1985). Many individuals turn to AA because of family problems. Embarrassing or harmful incidents involving loved ones contributed to my motivation to attend an AA meeting. Many members attended the first AA meeting at the insistence of spouses, parents, or significant others. Most said this initial attendance had very little effect. While many individuals turned to AA for help because of problems in the home, members stressed that if they initially attended "for somebody else, because they wanted me to go," it did little to alleviate the problem. Most maintained, "I had to do it for myself, because I wanted it."

In many cases, members stress that they simply could not continue to harm close family members and friends with their "alcoholic behavior." One woman experimented and rejected AA for years, but finally she "began working the program" after an uncontrolled, overreaction to a disturbance by her grandchildren. "I just don't want to go on hurting the people I love the most." After almost two years "this time" in the program she has almost one year of continuous sobriety. Another woman began attending meetings of AA for the first time because her five-year-old daughter had begun to question her about her drinking. She recalled that her mother is an alcoholic and that she didn't want to continue the "charade" of drinking constantly and trying not to let it become known to her small child. This woman's husband had been told by a doctor that due to his diabetes he shouldn't drink, but she got no support from him, and he continued to drink and consistently tried to persuade her to have a drink with him. Competition with AA from a spouse is common and mitigates against continued affiliation. The lack of support and strong indications that she attended for her daughter's sake caused her commitment to waiver. She dropped out of the program after maintaining her abstinence for two months. These cases are representative of many members of AA. Repeated experiences in which they found themselves out of control or unable to adequately explain drunken behavior to loved ones convinced them to seek help. The first woman went to AA many times and dropped out before she abandoned the idea that she could control herself when drinking. The second, younger woman, due to a lack of harmful personal incidents and the unsupportive nature of her most significant other, abandoned AA and the goal of abstinence as a way of life. Members of the group tend to believe that "she'll be back."

Ablon (1984) has done significant work dealing with the family experience of alcoholism. Due to shifting patterns of social organization in contemporary American culture, she has defined the family to include any significant others in the lives of alcoholics, whether or not they live in the same household. This is reflected in many members' problems with boyfriends, girlfriends, and other friends who eventually led them to believe that they needed the help of AA. Members agreed that as a result of alcoholism they caused family members, spouses, offspring, and significant others to whom they were unrelated by blood or marriage great difficulties.

Many members "lost" their families as a result of their drinking. They became estranged from families and significant others, yet continued to drink. Most found new "friends" that liked to drink. The preferred companion enjoyed drinking more and behaved worse than they did. These drinking relationships were substituted for primary relationships that had been "lost" as a direct consequence of drinking. Although this provided a sense of social membership, people in AA describe such personal interactions as unsatisfying. Rather than continued drinking with these other groups, many members of this study became more socially isolated as the condition developed. Finally, most said they preferred to drink alone. As one member said, "It was more and more just me and drinking in that room. It got so bad that I would look around when I left the house to make sure there was nothing laying out that would be embarrassing if I died. Everything just closed in more and more until there I was . . . in the box."

As the progression led to increased solitary drinking for most, they began to feel increasingly separated from other people. In an effort to deal with such isolation, almost all reported an increase in drinking. Only when they were drinking did they feel "connected" to anything. Just as they had learned that drinking could make them feel more a part of a social situation in which they were timid, insecure, or uncomfortable, they also learned that they could gain some warped sense of belonging, even in isolation, through the use of alcohol. Ultimately, just as alcohol had "quit working" for them as a "social lubricant," it quit working as an anaesthetic. It failed to ease the pain, suffering, and all-encompassing futility of drunken isolation. Most individuals who come to the program and accept abstinence as a solution are suffering from significant social estrangement at the very least. More commonly, they suffer from thorough social isolation. As one member stated, "At first my family and friends suggested I *shouldn't* drink so much, then they asked me *not* to drink so much, then they asked me *not to come around* when I had been drinking *so* much. Finally, they told me to just *not* come around."

EMPLOYMENT AND FINANCIAL PROBLEMS

The inability to function on the job or maintain consistent employment due to missed work, poor production, or bad relations with supervisors or co-workers influenced many individuals to become active AA participants. Some maintained jobs and paid the bills, but had interpersonal problems in the work place. Consistently employed individuals often found the financial basis of living undermined by the increased use of alcohol and intoxicated states. Even though many held jobs and should have enjoyed sufficient income, the subjects of this study said they spent excessively on drinking related activities, and they were thus short of money to meet basic, financial obligations, such as food, housing, medical and dental care, and transportation. Although they earned decent money, they were deficient in self-care (Levin 1987). Alcohol and the altered states it produced had become the priority.

The subjects in this study overwhelmingly indicated this description was simply the first stage of employment and financial difficulties in the progression of their alcoholism. Most alcoholics do not recognize such early signs. As one member put it, "I thought the biggest problem was that I wasn't making enough money." They continued to drink and to resent employers. Some tried to change the situation by changing jobs. Others worked harder in hope of promotion, advancement, and a higher salary. The failure to improve and alleviate such problems led to more intensive self-medication (Khantzian 1990). It was a vicious circle.

Stories of the members of Alcoholics Anonymous make clear that despite these early developments, they increasingly depended on alcohol. Most continued alcoholic development into an ever-tightening spiral of despair—a process that constitutes a physical, mental, emotional, financial, and spiritual descent (Brown 1985). By the time they arrived in AA, members were generally underemployed, unemployed, or at the very least were having substantial difficulties in their work. Some had lost very good jobs and others were barely hanging on to a livelihood or vocation (Bissell and Haberman 1984, Levin 1987, Madsen 1974).

PHYSICAL AND MENTAL HEALTH

Chronic, heavy drinking causes life-threatening illnesses and conditions. Despite diagnosis and warnings, most alcoholics continue to drink. Some members were educated intensively and repeatedly regarding the consequences of drinking. Physicians, psychiatrists, and other health professionals cautioned them, but they were unable to discontinue the use of alcohol. Most members regard this total inability to care for oneself as a dramatic and accurate demonstration of the "insanity of alcoholism."

Some members came very close to death by illness, others suffered life threatening accidents, and almost all testify "that but for the grace of God I would have been dead a long time ago" due to intoxicated behavior. Hangovers, poor dietary habits, lack of proper rest, and the general deterioration of health are associated with deficiencies in self-care. These were important factors in many members' decision to go to AA. Most members said they were "sick" when they "walked through the doors of AA."

Almost all members maintain, in addition to being physically ill, that they suffered extreme emotional distress. Most plead insanity. Anxiety, depression, fear, anger, rage, jealousy, envy, greed, and resentment were some of the more prevalent feelings by which they were victimized (Gallant 1987). Most individuals finally came to AA for help when they were overpowered by the "Hideous Four Horsemen—Terror, Bewilderment, Frustration, Despair" (AA 1976: 151). They felt they needed to be healed.

QUANTITY AND QUALITY OF PROBLEMS

Most members cite specific events involving the law, family relations, employment, finances, and health that led them to accept participation in AA as an alternative to drinking. The overwhelming majority of members admit to problems in many of these areas. Through the sheer weight of the empirical evidence, gathered through personal experience over a long period of time and manifest in repeated behavioral problems related to their alcohol use, they came to believe they could not continue. Everything in their existence was falling down around them. Many of them considered suicide as a solution. A few attempted to kill themselves. Even those who had never attempted suicide often considered the benefits of being dead. As one member frequently stated about why he came to AA, "I didn't mind the idea of dying, but it was just taking so long." Many referred to their alcoholism as "suicide on the installment plan."

Considering the dramatically increased likelihood of an alcoholic's committing suicide compared with members of the general population (Gallant 1987), such stories are not difficult to believe. Through these combined hardships, members of Alcoholics Anonymous were "completely beaten down" by their experience. They were ready to "surrender." These severe wounds are characterized by Levin, "Years of drinking have left residual scars in all areas of the alcoholic's life; vocational, financial, interpersonal, and intrapsychic" (1987: 220). He also states that in the diagnosis and treatment of alcoholism, "The essential characteristic of alcoholic drinking is its *compulsiveness* [italics added]. The drinker continues to drink regardless of the consequences to health, relationships, emotional stability, and of financial well-being" (1987: 43). Most members claimed that they realized they had problems with alcohol long before they sought a solution in AA, but they denied that they were alcoholics.

Most attempted to discontinue or minimize their drinking on their own. They could not. The periodic drinkers underwent periods of abstinence to reassure themselves that they were not alcoholics. After a few days, weeks, months, and even years of abstinence, they would be confident they were not alcoholic, but they all returned to problem drinking and related behaviors. The vast majority of the members' experience in this study suggest that any attempt by the "real" alcoholic to return to drinking will ultimately fail. This predictable failure is considered a fact of experience in AA and is strongly supported in research (Madsen 1974, Vaillant

1983, Gallant 1987, Levin 1987, Moos et al. 1990). Although members said they made countless decisions to "quit drinking," they were never successful. Most believed they could resume their drinking and "not get in so much trouble this time," but they could not. Most members experienced such disasters repeatedly before they came to AA. Usually, they were able to "drink successfully" for only a short time. Eventually, they would always lose control.

LOSS OF CONTROL

Generally speaking, virtually all AA members experienced not only loss of control of their drinking, but loss of control over their own lives. In both cases, the loss of control is represented by members as progressive. Most claimed that they gradually lost control of first their drinking, then their lives. Many said their lives were always out of control and drinking was a way of managing their feelings about life. They often used alcohol to manage stress, feelings, depression, and problems. They came to a point at which they ceased to have any choices in their lives. This was particularly true of the choice of whether or not to drink. For most it became an obsession. Not the obsession of the craving, physically addicted, demented maniac, but the obsessive, compulsive urge to say, "Fuck it, I need a drink."

The importance of loss of control in the diagnosis of alcoholism, as well as the definition of alcoholism has been well documented (Brown 1985). While most studies recognize this aspect as an integral part of the syndrome, some have suggested that it is our own cultural premium on self-control that has assigned this aspect of the condition a more important role than it deserves (Room 1984). Room suggested that self-control is positively regarded as a personality trait in American culture, and investigators may have a bias concerning the concept and those people who cannot control themselves. This is no reason to disregard the fact that many recovering alcoholics recognize loss of control as the essential element in their drinking that leads them to believe they are alcoholics. It is also one of the primary causes of seeking abstinence. According to the data gathered from the members of AA in this study, loss of control must be considered as one general fact of life for practicing alcoholics. Alcoholics in AA frequently refer to the bewilderment they felt as practicing alcoholics. This feeling is centered on the inability to control their drinking or their lives. They frequently stated how humiliated and guilty they felt about not being in control and how they let their family, friends, employers, and co-workers down because they could not control themselves.

Self-control is considered to be an incredibly desirable quality in modern America. Through self-control we are supposed to be able to discipline ourselves in school, military service, family, employment, and other important areas to accomplish our goals and succeed in life. Most alcoholics in AA repeatedly experienced loss of control of their behavior when drinking and were emotionally devastated by the consequences (Madsen 1974). They feel this loss progressively worsened and became extremely debilitating. They were completely unable to rationally explain how they could continue to engage in drinking behavior given the problems it repeatedly caused. So they denied it.

DENIAL: "I AM NOT AN ALCOHOLIC"

Generally, most alcoholics who participate in AA have had ample experience with the use of alcohol that negatively impacted their ability to maintain adequate relations with families, employers, and the legal system. It is largely true that most of these people thought that loss of control was one of their primary problems. Loss of control and the unmanageability of their lives caused a great deal of suffering. The other general truth, as expressed by most in this study, is that they continued to deny that they were alcoholics in the face of massive evidence to the contrary.

Folk conceptions of the prototypic alcoholic as a wino and skid row bum, and of alcoholism as a moral defect that evidences a weakness of willpower, contribute significantly to the necessity of denial. Many members knew they had problems when they drank, but they thought it was because they had too much that night, or because they were upset over their job, girlfriend, boyfriend, husband, wife, mother, father, Reagan, Bush, or Clinton—and not because they were alcoholics. Members stressed that for years they felt that if they could satisfy the other troublesome aspects of their lives, they wouldn't have so many problems with alcohol because they would be happy.

It is a real chicken-or-egg, which-came-first-type of controversy, not only to professionals engaged in the study of alcoholism, but to the individuals who suffer. Most people in AA admitted denying that alcohol was a problem and wanted to believe that it was only a symptom of the other difficulties in life. Some health care professionals may have a tendency to accept, promote, and treat alcoholics based on this assumption. However, virtually all AA members in this study said that they had to accept that *"ALCOHOL WAS THE PROBLEM."* After some time in recovery, they began to grasp in what ways it was only a symptom, but first the alcohol had to go (Bissell and Haberman 1984). In recovery they began to recognize that they had no clue about how to live. Most AA members' approach to this concern is truly bio-psycho-social (Wallace 1983). Members accepted that there may be a disease condition from which they suffer, but they admitted that they made things worse through their willful choice to deny that a problem existed. They all agreed that they had to remove the alcohol before they could address other problems.

Almost all practicing alcoholics deny that they are alcoholic. Some may admit the problem, but deny there is any solution and continue drinking regardless of the consequences. Harris (1989) describes such an individual in a discussion of the medical *and* moral explanations that people need to deal with disease and injury. She encountered a repeatedly hospitalized alcoholic patient who showed the despair and hopelessness of an individual who had accepted alcoholism as a part of God's will for his life. Denial is the vanguard of countless individual alcoholics who continue to suffer, deteriorate, and lose hope.

AMERICAN CULTURE AND THE DEVELOPMENT OF ALCOHOLISM

Almost all members of Alcoholics Anonymous acknowledge that they suffer from some sort of a disease. The extent to which they believe it is a bio-genetic predisposition to the development of alcoholism varies considerably. Some members accept a simplistic explanation of a pathological "allergy." Most are somewhat more aware of scientific explanations that have ruled out many such proposed metabolic differences, but nonetheless they indicate that there may be heritable factors that lead to the development of the problem. However, very few rely exclusively on a pathological disease model as an explanation for their alcoholism, and a few completely reject the idea of alcoholism as a disease. Generally, they recognize alcoholism as a three-fold affliction of the body, mind, and spirit. It is clear from the experience of subjects in this study that they think their alcoholism developed primarily because of the "old ideas" in which they believed, regardless of whether or not they believe alcoholism is a pathological illness. As many said, "I was an alcoholic just waiting to happen. All I had to do was add the alcohol."

Members believe that the values, attitudes, and beliefs they acquired as participants in American culture contributed significantly to the cause of their sickness. George and Louise Spindler (1983) identified the basic concepts of individualism, achievement orientation, equality, conformity, sociability, honesty, competence, optimism, work, and authority as pivotal beliefs and values that constitute a kind of American cultural ideology. The interaction of all these concepts in the introduction and integration of the individual into the drinking culture, the development of alcohol dependence, and the process of recovery is described by members of Alcoholics Anonymous as a part of the "old ideas."

Individualism and an achievement orientation do not head the list of beliefs and values that are pivotal to American cultural ideology by chance. As children we begin to learn that each person is a unique and important being, and many of us are indulged to a great extent. Most of us learn that we can get what we want by demanding it rigorously enough, and through wailing and whining we often are able to satisfy every whim. This is the nature of nurturing. Some of us who are not as intensely "spoiled" in this manner are generally taught that the world waits at our feet if we can only achieve our potential. Some of us less fortunate, who live in abject poverty and hopelessness are taught that we have to look out for ourselves because no one else will, that life is unfair, and if we want something, it has to be taken at the first opportunity. Usually, these three lessons are variably synthesized as an important part of our system of beliefs *regardless* of socioeconomic status.

The need to preserve and enhance the self is a necessary prerequisite to continued life on this planet as individuals, as groups, and as a species, but in American culture we have taken it to a higher level. The material abundance made available by our science, technology, and economy have made it possible to enjoy riches beyond the wildest dreams of the people who have, until the recent past inhabited this earth. Members of Alcoholics Anonymous identify the unrealistic expectations they had in regard to the possibilities of ever-greater affluence and all manner of self-gratification as important motivations in life and in their drinking.

Virtually all members of Alcoholics Anonymous said that they began to drink in an effort to be a part of the crowd. Peer pressure to drink alcohol can be enormous to the adolescent and the adult alike. Despite the massive problems that have been identified by the legal, social, and health care systems, alcohol enjoys a positive reputation as a social lubricant. We are urged by the people in our lives and through advertising to drink in order to conform to the expectations of others. We are encouraged to enter into a spirit of conviviality that the drug fosters. Adolescents experience this pressure as a dare to become adult and as a rite of passage. Adults in the work place experience this pressure as an invitation to be one of the crowd, and business people experience this pressure as an adequate expression of themselves as suitably refined. Thus we drink to be accepted as equals by others.

Recovering alcoholics in AA claim that this is the essential mechanism by which they were enculturated into the drinking culture. Although their stories indicate a high degree of variability, almost all said that they loved the togetherness that they experienced in drinking environments. Alcohol worked. They no longer felt separated or in any way less than everyone else; instead they felt themselves to be an integral part of the social scene. It conquered their anxiety, loosened their tongues, and made them able to joyously share this experience with others. They no longer felt ugly, stupid, or weak, but felt sexy, intelligent, and sufficiently powerful. It heightened their sense of personal, vocational, and/or professional competence in relation to others. The only trouble was that eventually it quit working.

As alcohol became ineffective as a social lubricant, they began to experience difficulty. They could no longer achieve the release to proper sociability in order to conform to the expectations of others. They lost the sense of equality. They tried repeatedly to recapture the essence of the experience of belonging by drinking more alcohol, but the lack of control over the intake of alcohol, and the lack of control over behavior that resulted as a side effect of intoxication made them even less sociable and less able to conform to the expectations of those around them. This led to admonitions that they shouldn't drink so much and they shouldn't behave as they had. Not only did it destroy their sense of equality through the lack of social integration, but eventually it devastated their sense of individual self-esteem.

They redoubled their efforts to correct the situation by increasing their reliance on alcohol and they reported this strategy had serious side effects. They became more grandiose in their expectations of themselves and others. Optimistically, they sought to show those around them that they were competent as individuals, workers, professionals, and drinkers of alcohol. They worked harder and faster in an effort to demonstrate an ability to handle all these aspects of life on their own, but they were not successful, especially in drinking alcohol. Although they tried to control themselves and their alcohol intake, they could not. This led to a deepening sense of failure.

Failure is not a concept that we value in American society. We are taught that if "at first you don't succeed, try, try, again," but we are not taught to concede failure. Most alcoholics in AA said that they followed this prescription until they "hit bottom." They could not accept the failure to control their own destiny or realize the things that they wanted to achieve. But perhaps the worst disappointment expressed by subjects in this study was the failure to "drink successfully." Drinking should be so simple, enjoyable, and advantageous. The failure to control their drinking was an absolutely devastating failure. The inability to exercise the self-control that is a critical aspect of the concepts of individuality and personal achievement was totally unacceptable. Everybody drinks. So they applied themselves and worked even harder to control drinking and life in order to convince themselves, their families, and their friends that they could handle life through their own persistence and willpower.

But, when someone asked them how much they had had to drink, the answer invariably became "just a couple of beers" or "just a couple of drinks." They became dishonest about how much they drank. At first, they began to hide the extent of their drinking, and later they began to hide it completely, as far as that was possible. Many of them had to call in sick to work as a result of hangovers and lack of sleep. Family members were encouraged to assist in the cover-up. And they continued to lie to themselves as well, for they maintained that others were responsible for the unhappiness that drove them to such extremes.

Living this lie, they ignored the fact that they were incapable of sociability and conformity in regard to the expected behavior associated with alcohol use. They disregarded the fact that they were dishonest with themselves and everyone with whom they were in contact. They refused to acknowledge the fact that their competence as workers, business people, professionals, and viable family members was questionable. In the spirit of perseverance and optimism that we so highly esteem, they denied their problem was alcoholism and sought to change their behavior on their own. In accordance with the values of American culture, they also rejected any authority over their use of alcohol or over their lives. It is interesting to note that "authority" is the only pivotal belief that was identified by Spindler and Spindler (1983) as having a basically negative value in American cultural ideology. However, it is not unexpected, given the high premium that we place on individualism and achievement.

The American mythology is basically one in which a human being, through an act of personal will and power, tames the wild natural forces that are set against the individual. People are also expected to tame other human forces that are set against them, and in the context of our mythology, authority is often one of the forces that must be overcome. The corrupt sheriff, politician, or robber baron is slain and the hero presides over a new social and personal truth. The legacy of racism, the history of the labor union movement, and the tragedy of the Vietnam War are just three examples of the value realized in the need to reject authority.

Alcoholics in Alcoholics Anonymous paint a picture of their behavior in this respect that makes the most radical, rebellious behavior a case for conformity. Virtually all claim to have had no respect for any authority. They rejected the authority of the legal system that sometimes incarcerated them for behavior due to intoxication. They rejected the authority of the professionals in the health care system that suggested they would continue to suffer and perhaps even die if they continued to drink. They rejected the authority of the social system that banned them from countless drinking establishments. They also rejected the authority of religious institutions that suggested they could be helped by living a more religious life. And they rejected the authority of loved ones who suggested that they were not satisfying the duties and responsibilities of kinship.

Alcoholics in AA said that they rejected such authority primarily because it interfered with the conception of themselves as capable, independent, worthwhile individuals. They wanted to believe that they could control their drinking and their lives. They wanted to believe that they were self-reliant and self-sufficient human beings. They wanted to believe that they didn't need help, and they didn't want to believe that they were dependent on anything or anyone. They wanted to believe that they were competent to live up to the idealized behaviors that were suggested as reality by the dominant American cultural ideology. It is clear that the conflict between these pivotal beliefs and values and the inability to realize these ideals in their lives substantially contributed to the systemic cycle of despair that is so characteristic of the practicing alcoholic.

AFFILIATION WITH ALCOHOLICS ANONYMOUS

Based on observations made in the course of this study, the individual most likely to affiliate with Alcoholics Anonymous in order to achieve sobriety has had significant behavioral problems as a result of loss of control, or an inability to control the intake of alcohol. Due to the loss of control, they have experienced difficulties with most primary interpersonal and institutional interactions. The intensity and seriousness of these problems became so unbearable that members were eventually compelled to "surrender" their denial. For many this took years and for some, decades. Members often expressed feeling mentally, physically, and spiritually "bankrupt" when they finally accepted affiliation with AA as a solution.

Acknowledging the existence of the problem is the first real step to recovery. Step 1 of the AA program, "We admitted we were powerless over alcohol, that our lives had become unmanageable," summarizes the process that leads to affiliation. When they abandoned denial of the problem and turned to AA for help, many members felt they essentially, "Came to believe only a power greater than ourselves could restore us to sanity" (step 2). For most members, it was not a "conversion" experience per se, but a simple, significant admission that they needed help. They sought assistance from the AA group, which was the only "higher power" many newcomers were willing to consider when they initially come to Alcoholics Anonymous.

Many members said they rejected AA initially because they could not accept the fact that they could not heal themselves. Self-reliance is another extremely important, highly regarded value in American culture. It is an aspect of the same system of beliefs that places self-control upon a pedestal. It is a part of the old, "pulled myself up by my bootstraps," Horatio Alger mentality that anything can be accomplished if, "I set my mind to it." It is an underlying belief and confidence in the power of the self. Dependence is the antithesis of this belief and to depend on others is to be humiliated in this system of values generated by the American cultural experience. Most members of AA felt that they should be self-sufficient and not have to depend on anyone else for anything.

Before coming to AA, members thought that they should be able to quit drinking or cut down by virtue of their own personal power. Most felt that they needed to do it on their own in order to maintain a self-respecting independence. Ironically, they had increasingly imposed on family, friends, and anyone else unfortunate enough to come in close contact to help them with the financial, emotional, physical, and psychological consequences of their alcoholism. Most only had an illusion of self-reliance and consistently needed assistance due to the inability to manage their own lives. But the exigency of independence in the ego structure made denial a continuing necessity. To admit to alcoholism was to admit that they couldn't control themselves and that they were dependent. Most stated that when they finally came to accept the solution provided by AA, they did not know how they could recover, but they had finally become convinced they could not accomplish it on their own.

Some members sought treatment and others were directed through various interventions. Almost all members talk of initial exposure to a treatment alternative and a return to drinking. Some entered inpatient treatment facilities and mental hospitals. Some went to Alcoholics Anonymous. Others sought the help of physicians and psychiatrists. Others talked of relocating to live with other relatives or the attempt to effect other "geographic cures." In the beginning, none of these things accomplished much abstinence for most of the individuals in this study. It was only the gradual acceptance of the necessity of assistance that ultimately led to recovery.

The role of denial and the inability to accept the fact that they are alcoholics is of crucial importance. Even though many of them were in sad shape and knew that they had a problem, they could not entertain the idea of suffering from alcoholism. Many of them had numerous contacts with the health care community, which proved to be of no avail. This is not an indictment of the health care system. As one member said, "I saw a lot of psychiatrists and they were of no help whatsoever. Of course, I lied to them about everything, especially my drinking, so they really didn't have a chance." The therapist often had little good information on which to base a diagnosis and suggest treatment.

All members spoke of the hopelessness they experienced as a result of these attempts. There are also many people who first "got sober" in an inpatient therapeutic environment that either utilized an AA type approach and/or encouraged AA attendance as a part of their outpatient aftercare. Some were referred to Alcoholics Anonymous by a physician or psychologist. Many of these members went to AA for a while and returned to drinking, only to show up at AA again later. A few members stayed in recovery after the first experience. However, most of the subjects in this study talked of many false starts. When they finally "hit bottom" and were ready to try Alcoholics Anonymous, they went to a meeting.

4

The Meeting

The AA meeting is the basic tool of Alcoholics Anonymous and the fundamental setting for observations in this study. Since each group is autonomous except regarding matters that could affect AA as a whole, scheduling, topics, and the practical details of different meetings will vary, but the structure of the experience is basic and shared throughout AA culture in the United States. This similarity reflects the sense of community shared by members of Alcoholics Anonymous. The ritual and ceremonial structure of the meeting combined with a basic message centered on a system of beliefs is analogous to the celebration of Mass in the Roman Catholic church in this country. The shared attitudes, values, concepts, and beliefs are contained in the liturgy, as well as the ceremonial presentation itself, regardless of the location of the church. People are able to visit other churches outside the local community and are still able to share in a profound sense of belonging. Similarly, AA members often state that they can walk into a meeting anywhere in the country and hear people talking about the "things I need to hear."

In the early development of AA, it was common that individuals attempting to help others to recover would arrange a meeting once a week in the house of one of the members of the fellowship (AA 1976). Some members who were introduced to AA in the rural areas within the last 20 years said that one or two meetings a week is still the norm in many small towns. One woman who began going to AA in the city of Dallas 30 years ago said that when she first began to get sober they only had meetings scheduled on Friday and Saturday night and it could be a long week until the next meeting. Due to the tremendous growth of Alcoholics Anonymous in urban areas, this is no longer the case.

According to the "Dallas Metroplex Meeting Schedules: 1993–1994," compiled and distributed twice a year by the Dallas Intergroup Association of Alcoholics Anonymous, there were 1,239 meetings at 83 different group locations each week throughout the city, suburbs, and a few of the outlying communities. More groups and meetings have been established since that time. The overwhelming majority of these scheduled meetings are in the city and the immediate suburbs, and a few groups were not even listed or represented in this pamphlet. There are proportionately more meetings scheduled on Friday, Saturday, and Sunday than on Monday through Thursday. There are six groups that schedule 30 meetings or more per week, and 39 is the most scheduled in any one group for the weekly period. There are 21 groups that schedule 10 or fewer meetings per week. Ten of these groups are the only ones that meet in churches and most of them meet only once or twice a week. They are good examples of the formation of special groups to meet the particular needs of the AA community. There is even one group that meets at the World Trade Center. It schedules only one meeting a week, on Fridays, except during business markets, when there are a large number of people on site. During markets more meetings may be scheduled by out of town business people. Interested persons are directed to inquire at the front desk for meetings that may be scheduled during the markets. Although a few groups, such as those that meet in the churches or the Trade Center, may have space donated to them for the purpose of holding meetings, most of the groups in the local area raise enough money through their own contributions to rent space specifically for the purpose of maintaining an AA group.

Conservatively, there are approximately 150 daily meetings in the local area through the week and almost 200 meetings daily on Friday, Saturday, and Sunday. It is no longer necessary for the alcoholic attempting to recover to "white-knuckle it" during the week in order to arrive at the weekend to make a meeting of AA. There is ample opportunity to attend a meeting on a daily basis, usually without traveling too far from home or work. This frequency and locality facilitates greater attendance at meetings and significantly helps people to recover. This situation has systemically enhanced the success of Alcoholics Anonymous as a treatment alternative over the past 20 years. As more people turn to AA for help, more meetings and assistance are available.

I attended many meetings at various locations, which confirmed that there is a basic meeting structure and a complex and shared system of beliefs within Alcoholics Anonymous. One of the groups was touted by its officers and members as the largest, single AA group in the world. Over 100 people were observed in attendance on numerous occasions. Other groups varied in size. The larger groups generally had about 50- 75 individuals in attendance and the smaller groups as few as 10 to 20. AA members encourage each other to occasionally attend different groups, but most newcomers are counseled to find a group with which they feel comfortable, attend regularly, and make it their "home group." I followed this advice and became a regular member of a small, intimate, and eclectic club near my home. I attended numerous meetings in which there were only 5 to 10 people present and some with as many as 35. Generally, 15 to 25 people attend each meeting. It was in this small club that most of the observations for this study were made.

THE CLUB

Upon entering the south entrance of the club, it is obvious that this is not the richest or biggest AA group in the city, much less the world. The room is approximately 18 feet across and the walls seem dingy even with a fresh paint job. The furniture is old and worn; the tables are inexpensive and often dirty. It is and appears to be one of the oldest clubs around. Chairs alternate around the perimeter with tables so that everyone has somewhere to put the coffee, cigarettes, and ashtrays necessary to members' comfort. In the center of the room are three long tables that provide the auxiliary seating. Backs to the wall is the preferred position of most and these seats always fill up first. Latecomers have to sit in the middle of the room at one of the long tables.

Forty or so feet to the north end of the room is the podium. An old microphone stands cocked to one side atop the lectern and a sign adorns the front that reads in large letters, "BUT FOR THE GRACE OF GOD." Above it hangs a sign that informs those in attendance that "WE CARE." The wall behind the podium is draped with the Twelve Steps of Alcoholics Anonymous. Each step is written on a small, wooden looking, scroll shaped, paper plaque, giving them the appearance of something ancient and perhaps sacred. Below the steps, on the right side of the front wall is another larger, but similar presentation of the Serenity Prayer, which reads, "God grant me the serenity to accept the things I cannot change, the courage to change the things I can, and wisdom to know the difference."

A door stands open directly behind the speaker's lectern, through which a huge sign with the Lord's Prayer is partially visible from various positions in the room. To the left of the door, below the steps, is a bulletin board on which are hung various fliers, announcements from other clubs and conferences, cartoons from the newspaper, and a copy of this month's budget statement, according to which the club appears to be existing month to month, with little or nothing in reserve. On the far top left corner of this wall, almost obscured by an overhang is another sign that reads, "I am responsible. Whenever anyone anywhere reaches out for help, I want the hand of AA always to be there. And for that I am responsible." Just to the left is a sink and the coffee maker. On the coffee maker is a sign that reads, "Remember what it was like." On the counter is a small slot where people are asked to drop a contribution of a quarter a cup. But as one member says, "If you haven't got a quarter, go ahead and get your coffee, but if you do, we sure need it." This is a popular spot in which to congregate before and after meetings.

On the east wall, toward the front of the room, is a large chalkboard announcing members' anniversaries of abstinence or AA "birthdays" to be celebrated at the end of the month, a schedule of meetings and speakers for the week, and the "Thought for the Month," which is usually a quote from some passage of the Big Book of Alcoholics Anonymous. Next to that is another long, narrow, blackboard titled, "Motivation Board." There are 12 sections, beginning with one month at the bottom through 12 months at the top. There are always more names at the bottom than at the top, which reflects the attrition of newcomers. High above the motivation board is a small, unobtrusive sign that reads, "you are never a failure until you fail to try."

The middle of the wall features a large sign containing the Twelve Traditions. On each side of the traditions is a very large, old, photographic portrait of Bill W. on the left and Dr. Bob on the right. This is the only group I observed in which these portraits are present. It indicates the age and longevity of the club and the reverence that the co-founders of Alcoholics Anonymous were accorded by members in the past. In fact, one of the more senior members of the club is fond of saying that "we trained most of them over here," when discussing other groups that have been formed in the area. It is the old-timers who refer to Bill W. and Dr. Bob most often in discussions. On the west wall are the "On the Beam" and "Off the Beam" lists of characteristics, and scattered throughout the remainder of the room are signs that read, "First Things First, Live and Let Live, Easy Does It, But For the Grace of God, It's Ok to drink like a fish, as long as you drink what a fish drinks," and "Think, Think, Think." One sees when leaving the club, a small sign posted at eye level right next to the door-jam. It reads, "What you see here, what you hear here, let it stay here."

The first time that most members "walked through the doors of AA," all these things on the wall were a little bit weird. Although the particulars of each club are different, all have the steps, traditions, and various sayings on the wall, and all clubs observed in this study had a motivation board. The first time I walked through the doors of the club to attend a meeting of AA, I thought, these alcoholics are really strange. This place looks just like some dive, some joint a bunch of drunks would come to in order to get drunk. Later a member informed me that it had been a small neighborhood bar before it had become an AA club. Now the only drinking in the place is coffee and Cokes, the most abused substance is tobacco, and all the socializing and conviviality is based on abstinence and sobriety. Instead of going there to drink and enjoy a sense of belonging, people come to achieve and maintain sobriety and to enjoy the fellowship of an AA meeting.

"OPEN" OR "CLOSED" MEETINGS

Meetings of AA are usually designated as "open" or "closed." At open meetings anyone may attend. Family, members of the community, newspaper reporters, scientific observers, or anyone else is welcome. Closed meetings are limited to those who think they "have a problem with alcohol." This distinction is made to protect the anonymity of the individual alcoholic in AA and to limit intrusions into the intimate details regarding a person's problems with alcohol and their life by someone who is not an alcoholic.

AA members experience the tragedy of alcoholism on a very personal level. One of the basic principles of AA is that no one can understand the problems of the alcoholic like another alcoholic. It is with this belief, they encourage people with alcohol problems to share their feelings so that others who have had similar experiences may identify with them. As with any therapeutic environment, this exchange can only be effective in an atmosphere of trust. Many people in AA have experienced intervention by family or health professionals and continued to deny the accusation of others that they are alcoholic for long periods of time. When they finally come to AA, it is extremely important that they feel safe. The closed meeting is supposed to mitigate against inhibitions by excluding people who might not be able to identify with the problem. At the meetings I attended, it was difficult to discern any qualitative difference between the two types of meetings.

Generally, even open meetings were only attended by AA members. In the history and development of AA, alcoholics were frequently accompanied by spouses and children in order to support the individual in the process of recovery. Often, they would remain in a separate room of the house and share with each other the difficulties they encountered as a result of alcoholism in the family. This led to the development of Al Anon and Al Ateen as separate organizations. Today, there is much less accompaniment by close family members. However, the designated "open" meeting serves many individuals who would not attend an AA meeting, except at the insistence of a spouse or other person who is concerned about their problems with alcohol. Many other individuals deny the existence of an alcohol problem and since anyone may attend the open meeting, they do not have to admit that they are alcoholic in order to visit. In these ways, the open meeting helps to facilitate attendance by those people who are not ready to accept the label "alcoholic." But for most regular AA members there is very little difference in what they are willing to share in a meeting, whether it is open or closed. This trust is sometimes misplaced.

One man, 13 years sober, was reflecting on the topic of the "fellowship of AA" and stated that he had learned to be very careful of what he said in an "open" meeting of AA. He said that he had told a particularly embarrassing story at an open meeting, only to have this story cause him some difficulty when heard by a woman who was not even a member of AA. She was working on a school project and sitting in on the meeting. Unknown to him, she knew who he was, since she was the wife of a business associate. The past transgressions that he had so willingly shared at the meeting soon became common knowledge to a number of individuals whom he did not wish to know about this part of his past. He used this story to caution other members that they could be vulnerable at "open" meetings if they discussed their very personal problems.

During the course of this study, I never heard another member caution regular members, even in the context of an open meeting. However, his story emphasizes that since those meetings are open to anyone, there may be someone in attendance who may be unaware of the concept of anonymity that is of critical importance to most AA members. Some people, such as news reporters, students, or scientific researchers, may be aware of the importance of anonymity to people in AA, but they may have their own agenda. They may ignore such restrictions for their own benefit, whether or not it may possibly cause harm to someone they don't even know and will ever see again. Incidents such as this are indicative of the reason why Alcoholics Anonymous is so very unavailable to most "outsiders" and so difficult for researchers to gain access and study. Obviously, some of the members' more personal experiences are most appropriately shared at "closed" meetings.

"SPEAKER" OR "DISCUSSION" MEETINGS

Meetings in AA can also be categorized by whether they are "speaker" meetings or "discussion" meetings. The speaker meeting usually features one person who tells a story of "what it was like before, what happened, and what it is like now." These stories can be viewed as examples of *myth* (Leavitt 1974), *folklore* (O'Reilly 1988), the *enculturation process* (Marrus 1988), *worldview* (Smith 1991), and *discourse* (Chrouser 1990). They have also been criticized as predictable rags-to-riches sagas that are invariably upbeat and unrealistically rosy, "if you don't use alcohol." But the fact that things were terrible and they got a lot better when sober is a reality for most recovering alcoholics. However, while the general structure of "what it was like before, what happened, and what it is like now" may be necessarily similar and predictably optimistic regarding the "alcohol focus," periodically hears speakers who are recently sober, depressed, and bewildered about the rest of their life without alcohol. People tell these stories in an effort to be honest and open about their past. Sometimes, an individual in early sobriety is encouraged to speak prematurely and makes a somewhat too revealing confession from the podium. This can have unhealthy emotional consequences and is one of the risks of well-intended, but ineffective "sponsorship."

Most of the speakers heard during the period of this study were well established in abstinence with at least one or two years in the program. Sometimes very experienced people told these stories and were very professional. Sometimes speakers were very nervous and had never spoken before a group of people. The listener has to suffer along with the speaker for an hour, but concentration on what they have to say and the human variability and similarity are the aspects of the story that are critical to the AA member. Learning to listen closely and nonjudgementally is an important part of the recovery process.

In addition to the one hour solo speaker meeting, there are also 12-step studies, which are usually given over the course of a month. During this four to five week period one speaker returns for an hour each week to tell how he or she has personally "experienced the steps of Alcoholics Anonymous." Each individual approaches the steps from his or her own personal experience and tries to relate to the group in attendance he or she "lives the steps." Many of those who present step studies remark that they present the steps differently every time. Most of these people have years of sobriety and many of them are asked constantly to speak at different groups. The most prepared and professional of these individuals are playfully called "circuit speakers."

These are the two most frequently scheduled types of speaker meetings, but the people within each AA group can schedule any type of meeting in an attempt to meet what are perceived as specific needs of that particular AA community. Speaker meetings facilitate attendance by those who still deny they have an alcohol problem or by those who do not feel they are alcoholic. In the speaker format there is no pressure to reveal yourself in any way to the group. Individuals may attend, listen to the speaker, and make their own decisions about the similarities or differences in their personal experience. Furthermore, since many alcoholics have become seriously debilitated and isolated on an interpersonal level, the speaker meeting allows them to deal more effectively with the "fear" of an AA meeting.

Many individuals express reservations they had in the beginning and claim to have attended primarily speaker meetings at first. Some people don't feel the need to talk about their problems, don't want to make the effort to participate, and thus prefer speaker meetings. Most AA members participate in discussions, but they also find speaker meetings to be educational, enlightening, and entertaining. Many of these speakers approach the topic of alcoholism in their lives with a great deal of levity and are truly hilarious, at least to the alcoholic. Many non-alcoholic observers at AA meetings are horrified when they hear such terrible stories and fail to grasp the humor. They don't really know how the alcoholic thinks.

Discussion meetings are basically focus groups. They are moderated by a "chairperson" and address a variety of topics in which everyone will be asked to focus on a specific issue. The process of choosing a topic varies from group to group. At some groups the chair always chooses the topic At the club, the process is much more egalitarian, reflecting the small, intimate setting. The chair will usually ask, "Does anybody have a topic?" or "Does anybody have a burning desire?" Anyone may volunteer something to be discussed. This highly informal process was extremely fortuitous for the purpose of this research and for my own recovery. Many times I suggested the topic and was able to gather information regarding anything that I felt needed to be clarified for the purpose of research as well as the maintenance of my own abstinence and sobriety. I also chaired a considerable number of meetings in which I suggested the topic. If no one has a suggestion, someone may read some passage from the Big Book or other literature to "see if we can get a topic out of that." Often, after introducing the topic the chair will add that, "you can talk about anything you want to." Sometimes one of the 12 steps was discussed, and sometimes one of the broader, organizing principles or concepts of the belief system of AA was the topic for the meeting.

The general structure of the discussion meeting is one of restricted interaction. Most importantly, no one is required or forced to share information about themselves, their problems, or anything else. Lay people and researchers alike have suggested that such a requirement is a weakness of AA. It is simply not true. People introduce themselves and simply state that they want to listen. No one is forced to speak, although it is encouraged. Each willing individual is allowed to talk without interruption and "cross talk" is not allowed or at the very least, discouraged. The idea is to allow the individual to express what he or she needs to without worrying about being engaged in an argument or having to defend himself or herself in any way. This reflects the egalitarian structure of Alcoholics Anonymous. At times, it may be necessary for the chair to cut off someone, but generally members are allowed to ramble considerably. Some individuals are extremely and habitually long-winded, but most people practice restraint so that "everyone will get a chance to share."

Although not conversational, there is a great deal of interaction within the entire event. While the meeting is in progress, people are free and welcome to move around the room to get coffee, a paper towel, go to the bathroom or whatever. Years ago, I remember a sign by the coffee pot that said, "Please get your coffee before the speaker talks," or something to that effect, but that sign has been gone for years. As the discussion moves around the room, people will be stimulated by what others have had to say, and often something previously mentioned will be directly addressed from another person's perspective. Additions and objections to previous statements are common, but objections are usually, though not always, expressed more as reservations. At times a meeting can become very emotional. Sometimes newcomers can be overwhelmed and begin to weep. The same is true for regular members who have been sober for a while and may be dealing with some intense difficulty in life. More often than not, alcoholics in AA meetings approach drinking and recovery with a great sense of humor. As a result, many meetings are funny, relaxing, and educational. People in AA constantly promote the therapeutic effects of participating in the discussions.

In addition to general discussion meetings, most groups also schedule a Big Book study, which usually adheres to some type of discussion format. Some groups are more successful with these "studies," than others. "Women's" and "men's" meetings are common. "Beginner's" meetings, which address the first three steps of the program, are scheduled in many groups, and other specific audiences, such as couples and families in recovery, may be addressed if the community perceives a need for a particular forum.

RITUAL AND CEREMONIAL STRUCTURE OF THE AA MEETING

The beginning of almost every open meeting I attended over the inital three year period of this study was called to order by the chair with the following opening statement: "This is an open meeting of Alcoholics Anonymous. We are glad you are all here—especially newcomers. In keeping with our singleness of purpose and our third tradition which states that 'the only requirement for AA membership is a desire to stop drinking,' we ask that all who participate confine their discussion to their problems with alcohol." This is followed by a recitation of the AA preamble:

Alcoholics Anonymous is a fellowship of men and women who share their experience, strength, and hope with each other that they may solve their common problem and help others recover from alcoholism. The only requirement for membership is a desire to stop drinking. There are no dues or fees for AA membership; we are entirely self-supporting through our own contributions. AA is not allied with any sect, denomination, politics, organization or institution; does not wish to engage in any controversy, neither endorses or opposes any causes. Our primary purpose is to stay sober and to help other alcoholics to achieve sobriety. (AA 1947)

This opening statement summarizes the Twelve Traditions (AA 1981) of AA. Essentially, it is an organizational statement made to welcome and assure the newcomer that the only purpose is sobriety, the only requirement is a "desire to stop drinking," that there are no fees, and that AA is not pushing any specific religion, politics, or other institutional agenda. It is designed to allay a newcomer's fears of

AA. Equally important, it is an organizational statement that seeks to remind members of these same principles.

In the case of a "closed" meeting, the opening statement begins somewhat differently, "This is a closed meeting of Alcoholics Anonymous. In support of AA's singleness of purpose, attendance at closed meetings is limited to persons who have a desire to stop drinking. If you think you have a problem with alcohol, you are welcome to attend this meeting. We ask that when discussing our problems, we confine ourselves to those problems, as they relate to alcoholism." The remainder of the opening statement is the same AA preamble. It is important to recognize that attendance at closed meetings is not restricted to alcoholics, but rather those who think they "have a problem with alcohol." Researchers often criticize AA for "forcing" people to accept an "alcoholic" identity in order to participate (Levinson 1983). This is not true, as this qualifying statement makes clear. It is up to the individual to decide whether or not the label is accurate. Many people attend AA on a trial basis, but not all these individuals are alcoholic. Some of them solve their problem without AA. Many reject the label of alcoholic in the beginning, but after recovery begins to develop they gradually come to accept the identity. The statement is also intended to remind AA members that what they see and hear in an AA meeting is confidential.

After reading the preamble, the chair always asked someone to read "How It Works" from Chapter 5 of the Big Book. The reading of this excerpt almost always takes place and is accorded a particular reverence by most active AA members.

HOW IT WORKS

Rarely have we seen a person fail who has thoroughly followed our path. Those who do not recover are people who cannot or will not completely give themselves to this simple program, usually men and women who are constitutionally incapable of being honest with themselves. There are such unfortunates. They are not at fault; they seem to have been born that way. They are naturally incapable of grasping and developing a manner of living which demands rigorous honesty. Their chances are less than average. There are those, too, who suffer from grave emotional and mental disorders, but many of them do recover if they have the capacity to be honest.

Our stories disclose in a general way what we used to be like, what happened, and what we are like now. If you have decided you want what we have and are willing to go to any length to get it—then you are ready to take certain steps.

At some of these we balked. We thought we could find an easier, softer way. But we could not. With all the earnestness at our command, we beg of you to be fearless and thorough from the very start. Some of us have tried to hold on to our old ideas and the result was nil until we let go absolutely.

Remember that we deal with alcohol—cunning, baffling, powerful! Without help it is too much for us. But there is One who has all power—that One is God. May you find Him now! Half measures availed us nothing. We stood at the turning point. We asked His protection and care with complete abandon.

Here are the steps we took, which are suggested as a program of recovery:

1. We admitted we were powerless over alcohol—that our lives had become unmanageable.
2. Came to believe that a Power greater than ourselves could restore us to sanity.

3. Made a decision to turn our will and our lives over to the care of God as we understood Him.

4. Made a searching and fearless moral inventory of ourselves.

5. Admitted to God, to ourselves, and to another human being the exact nature of our wrongs.

6. Were entirely ready to have God remove all these defects of character.

7. Humbly asked Him to remove our shortcomings.

8. Made a list of all those we had harmed, and became willing to make amends to them all.

9. Made direct amends to such people wherever possible, except when to do so would injure them or others.

10. Continued to take personal inventory and when we were wrong promptly admitted it.

11. Sought through prayer and meditation to improve our conscious contact with God as we understood Him, praying only for knowledge of His will for us and the power to carry that out.

12. Having had a spiritual awakening as a result of these steps, we tried to carry this message to alcoholics, and to practice these principles in all our affairs.

Many of us exclaimed, "What an order! I can't go through with it." Do not be discouraged. No one among us has been able to maintain anything like perfect adherence to these principles. We are not saints. The point is, we are willing to grow along spiritual lines. The principles we have set down are guides to progress. We claim spiritual progress rather than spiritual perfection.

Our description of the alcoholic, the chapter to the agnostic, and our personal adventures before and after make clear three pertinent ideas:

(a) That we were alcoholic and could not manage our own lives.

(b) That probably no human power could have relieved our alcoholism.

(c) That God could and would if He were sought. (AA 1976: 58–60)

The reading of "How It Works" is a definite contrast to the general organizational quality of the reading of the preamble. This reading is personal. It is a general statement to the individual listener that outlines the problem and the solution. Alcohol is "cunning, baffling, and powerful," and the individual is hopeless to control the compulsion to drink. A program of surrender, contrition, and restitution is the solution.

For many newcomers the reading of "How It Works" is about the last thing they hear in their first meeting of AA. The references to God, the authoritarian quality of the passage, and the Twelve Steps themselves generate incredible fear, resentment, and anger for the individual who still denies a problem with alcohol. Most are not ready to follow such suggestions, and virtually every individual involved in this study had to make repeated attempts to accept the program of AA as a solution to the problem of alcohol dependence. However, for those who are members of AA, follow the program, and have accepted this as a solution to their problem, this reading is accorded great respect as a very simple outline to a very simple program. Frequently, some statement in this passage is quoted as the basis for a topic of discussion.

After reading "How It Works," some groups read the Twelve Traditions. This is viewed by some as a long-winded restatement of the preamble, but others feel that it is as necessary as reading "How It Works."

TWELVE TRADITIONS

1. Our common welfare should come first; personal recovery depends on AA unity.
2. For our group purpose there is but one ultimate authority, a loving God as He may express Himself in our group conscience. Our leaders are but trusted servants they do not govern.
3. The only requirement for AA membership is a desire to stop drinking.
4. Each group should be autonomous except in matters affecting AA as a whole.
5. Each group has but one primary purpose—to carry its message to the alcoholic who still suffers.
6. An AA group ought never endorse, finance, or lend the AA name to any related facility or outside enterprise, lest problems of money, property, or prestige divert us from our primary purpose.
7. Every AA group ought to be fully self-supporting, declining outside contributions.
8. Alcoholics Anonymous should remain forever nonprofessional, but our service centers may employ special workers.
9. AA, as such ought never be organized; but we may create service boards or committees responsible to those they serve.
10. Alcoholics Anonymous has no opinion on outside issues; hence the AA name ought never be drawn into public controversy.
11. Our public relations policy is based on attraction rather than promotion; we need always maintain personal anonymity at the level of press, radio, and films.
12. Anonymity is the spiritual foundation of all our traditions, ever reminding us to place principles before personalities. (AA 1981)

Most of the meetings concluded this opening ritual, with the Serenity Prayer, "God, grant me the serenity to accept the things I cannot change, the courage to change the things I can and wisdom to know the difference." This is recited in unison by all who wish to participate after observing a moment of silence "for all those who are still out there suffering."

The scheduled business of the meeting now begins. If a speaker meeting, the person will be introduced and begin the talk. If a discussion meeting, the topic will be chosen and the discussion begins. Sometimes at the club, the chair will choose the first person to address the topic, point in the specific direction he or she wants to move around the room and say, "We'll just go around the room." Or the chair may move around the room in one direction calling the next person's name. Occasionally, the chair will jump around the room in no specific order. This seems to keep everyone on their toes. "Tag" meetings also keep everyone ready, since after "sharing" the member picks the next person to talk.

At the conclusion of the meeting, the "basket" is passed around the room while the group observes the seventh tradition and any AA related announcements may be solicited by the chair or offered from the floor. The chair will then extend the offer of a "desire chip," a small, metal token that represents the desire to quit drinking. If someone comes forward to accept a desire chip, he or she is met with rousing applause. After the meeting that person will almost invariably (in any club doing its job) be approached by one or more regular members. Some of the more aggressive AA members take the person aside and begin trying to convert him or her immediately. More often, a number of regular members may briefly introduce themselves, offer congratulations, and extend an invitation to come back.

Most groups will have a special "chip" night once a week or once a month to offer chips for various increments of sobriety. At the club it is a tradition to offer incremental chips of one, two, three, six, or nine months on a daily basis at the end of the 6:30 P.M. discussion meeting. Each person who comes forward to accept a chip gets a big round of applause and may get a pat on the back, handshake, or hug.

After the presentation of chips, the chair invites everyone who would like to participate to "close in the usual manner." At this everyone stands, joins hands, and is led in a recitation of the Lord's Prayer. This obvious, religious act taken directly from the Christian liturgy is often the last straw for many individuals attending their first AA meeting. This closing ritual was established by the early founders of Alcoholics Anonymous and has survived intact in the local area. There are other areas that have not maintained this practice. It has been reported in other parts of the country that some groups close with a recitation of the Serenity Prayer rather than the Lord's Prayer (Robertson 1988). This type of variation is entirely up to each AA group, which is "autonomous" except in matters affecting AA as a whole. Only one meeting I attended during the time of this research was concluded without a recitation of the Lord's Prayer.

This practice would appear to be contrary to the opening statement that AA "is not allied with any sect, denomination, politics, or organization." As an organization AA has admirably refrained from any such alignment. However, individuals within the fellowship are free to maintain such traditions as the recitation of the Lord's Prayer or to replace it with some other ritualized action more agreeable to the specific membership of a particular AA community, as some have done. Alcoholics Anonymous is not specifically a Christian community, and it encourages individuals who may hold other religious beliefs or no religious beliefs at all to adapt the principles of the 12-step program to their own beliefs and understanding. Proselytizing any specific religion in a meeting of AA is generally avoided by members. When some members insisted on getting too specifically religious, on numerous occasions other members were observed to object vehemently. As one member said one night at a meeting, "We're here to get sober, not to make everybody Christians." Alcoholics Anonymous is and should be open and useful to everyone regardless of religious affiliation, and a large proportion of members are not affiliated with any religious group.

The AA meeting is a highly stylized and ritualized event. It is ceremonially structured in order to reflect the common experience of the alcoholic in "practicing" alcoholism and in recovery. Although there may be variation in minor details, in most cases the event is remarkably similar everywhere. The reality of community and the attendant sense of belonging serves the population of urban American, recovering alcoholics very well. When one is faced with a new environment due to a change in employment or residence, AA presence and support still remain.

MEETINGS: ENVIRONMENT AND FUNCTION

The entire AA program revolves around the meeting. The first thing it provides to the individual seeking help with alcohol dependence is a place to go where no drinking is taking place and the people present are supportive of abstinence as a way of life. Most AA members remark on the importance of attending regularly. Members with longer periods of sobriety will often remark that when they don't go to enough meetings their "thinking gets all messed up" and they revert back to their "old ideas." For the newly abstinent individual who is alcohol dependent, frequent meetings are usually a welcome necessity.

As many people get sober in AA, they begin to realize how much time and effort they spent in drinking-related activities. The first thing many of these people have to do is replace the alcohol related activities. Meetings are the answer for many people. The individual, habituated to drinking everyday after work, initially has a lot of extra time in abstinence. Boredom can be a cruel enemy of the newly abtinent individual. Most claim they drank "over everything" and filled any empty time with alcohol and intoxication. Early in sobriety it is common for the new member to be assaulted constantly with the thought of drinking. This is particularly true when that person is faced with a lack of activity. The meetings are the activity that is recommended to deal with the past habit of taking a drink to fill the emptiness. Meetings are an effective way to short circuit the "mental obsession" that often follows the thought of taking a drink.

Although many AA members speak of being progressively isolated in their dependency on alcohol, for most alcoholics drinking begins and continues essentially as a social act. The social activity of the AA meeting replaces the social activity of drinking. Those who had become seriously isolated are provided with an environment in which to reintegrate themselves as social human beings. In any case, whether a person chooses to go to a speaker or discussion meeting and whether or not that person participates fully in such discussions is initially irrelevant. The most important thing is that he or she is present at a meeting of AA instead of drinking. "Suit up and show up" has been the topic of more than one meeting I have attended, and all such discussions stress the importance of returning to the alcohol focus as often as necessary in order to not take a drink.

AA members suggest to newcomers that they make "ninety meetings in ninety days," and if they don't like it, "we'll refund your misery." Some members went to meetings daily and sometimes more than once daily for as much as a year before they felt safe enough to be somewhere besides an AA meeting. Some talk about going by the meeting place at all hours of the day instead of giving in to the urge to take a drink and just sitting by themselves reading the things on the wall or finding "another alcoholic to talk to."

Alcoholics Anonymous can become simply a substitute dependency or "just another addiction." Addiction can be defined in many ways. It can refer to the compulsive need for habit-forming drugs or it can apply to many things that are external to the individual. Essentially, anything can become an addiction if the individual repeatedly seeks self-satisfaction and self-worth through the exterior "thing" he or she "must" have. Co-dependent people are addicted to the other person. Eating, jogging, and sex are three perfect examples of other possible addictions, but the key to the definition of addiction in the context of this study is that anything could become an addiction, if repeated use causes deleterious effects on the individual's physical or mental health (Imbach 1992). In some cases this can happen with AA, but even individuals who simple mindedly extend such addictive behavior by replacing alcohol with Alcoholics Anonymous have a much better chance to survive and live somewhat productive lives than if they were "practicing" their alcoholism. Most people in AA gradually limit their attendance in direct proportion to the amount of time they have been sober. At first the individual has to break the habit of drinking and almost constant attendance is one way that is achieved. As they begin to feel comfortable and direct their lives to other important and pressing matters, they spend less time going to meetings.

The meetings not only provide the scheduled program for the alcoholic, they also provide a social environment supportive of abstinence. Before meetings begin, people will interact in a more personal way. They also have the opportunity after the meeting has ended to engage in conversation in order to continue a discussion of a point that has surfaced in a meeting or simply to talk about their activities, jobs, families, fears, feelings, problems, triumphs, and the rest of their lives. Through these activities associated with AA meetings, they begin to share life with different people. They make new acquaintances and friends who share the common value of abstinence and sobriety. Through the meetings and the interpersonal activities attendant to them, alcohol dependent individuals are exposed to many people willing to share the experience of alcoholism. Meetings provide a place to go, support, ceremony, ritual, social activity, and despite criticism of the non-intellectual nature of the program of Alcoholics Anonymous, a rigorous intellectual frame of reference that has a direct bearing on the relationship of alcohol to the life of the individual who suffers from alcohol dependence (Kurtz 1979). The meeting is the basic mechanism of enculturation into the culture of Alcoholics Anonymous in America.

It is a paradox that the American cultural ideals that were corrupted in such a way as to help effect the enculturation of the alcoholic into the drinking culture and the subsequent development of alcohol dependence were also critical to the recovery of the alcoholics who participated in the meetings of Alcoholics Anonymous during the course of this study. All of the members said that after years of bitter struggle with alcohol, families, police, lawyers, doctors, psychiatrists, employers, and friends, they came to a point at which the entire structure of minimization, rationalization, and displacement that had supported the dependence on alcohol collapsed. Usually in a state of utter despair, they committed a deeply honest act. They admitted that they were powerless over alcohol and that their lives had become unmanageable, and they began attending meetings regularly. Such an honest admission, lovingly supported in the meetings by the AA community, was generally followed by a more honest appraisal of their past behavior, their relations with others, and themselves as selfish human beings who had little regard for anything except their own personal gratification. They began to abandon the grandiose self-image that had been constructed in support of the illusion which their lives had become. They realized that their efforts to conform to the ideal behaviors they believed were prescribed by American culture had been nothing but a delusion.

Many alcoholics arrived at such a state, went to a few AA meetings, and continued practicing their alcoholism. They were unable to accept the solution of Alcoholics Anonymous because they were unable to sustain the honest appraisal of themselves or they were unable to accept a program for living and believing that seemed to foster ideals so radically different from those in which they had been enculturated. As members continually said, "All you have to do is *change everything.*" For many people, this is too much to expect. They cannot give up everything they think they are. They cannot relinquish the idea that they are in control and personally powerful, as if they are God itself. Members said repeatedly that they had to give up the idea, "*I was God.*"

For those who "are ready" for the program of Alcoholics Anonymous, changes begin to occur. For some members, such changes came painfully slowly and for others, change occurred rapidly. As was read before every meeting in "How It Works," "If you want what we have, and are willing to go to any lengths to get it—then you are ready to take certain steps" (AA 1976: 58). In the meetings members always emphasized that the individual must be willing to do *anything* to achieve sobriety. The reason for this is apparent once it is clear that the total reorganization of the very beliefs with which one constructs reality is the target of transformation. This is often more than the average, American alcoholic can choke down. They may as well try to convince junk food freaks that broccoli, spinach, and carrots should be preferred foods. It is not only a challenge to what they feel sustains them, but also a challenge to what they want, crave, and think that they deserve.

The newcomer is immediately accepted and supported by the AA community with very little reservation. As long as they try to remain abstinent, they conform to other members' expectations and gain a new sociability. They are encouraged to not drink, come to meetings, and read the Big Book. If they do these things, they are optimistically reassured that "things *will* get better." As they work the steps of Alcoholics Anonymous, they achieve a sense of competence, not only with regard to abstinence, but also in the situations they face in daily life. As they reinterpret the world in AA, they truly begin to meet the idealized behavior of American culture. They endeavor to become more honest, more sociable, more competent, more able to work for what they want, more responsible for their actions, and more optimistic about the possible results. While these favorable changes may occur at a fairly rapid rate, newcomers are cautioned by members that the changes cannot last unless the *meaning* of the more important ideals of American culture are transformed as well. Newcomers are told that they must accept their limitations as human beings and submit to a power greater than themselves. It is relatively easy to modify one's behavior in relation to drinking and become more honest, sociable, competent, energetic, and optimistic as a result of not being intoxicated and out of control. However, it is more difficult to really change the way they think and believe about themselves in relation to the rest of the world.

The positive belief in the value of individualism, the achievement orientation, true equality, and the negative value of authority are the concepts that are most basic to the inner self and the most resistant to change. This is the real work of the 12-step program of Alcoholics Anonymous. Self-control, self-sufficiency, self-reliance, self-satisfaction, self-gratification, self-importance, and self-will are important corollaries to the American ideals of individualism and achievement and constitute a seven-headed monster that must be slain if the individual in the AA program is to succeed. Dependence is a concept in American culture that has an extremely negative value, but sober members of Alcoholics Anonymous maintain that the alcoholic attempting to recover has no alternative other than to accept dependence upon powers outside the scope and control of the self. They must learn to accept not only their human limitations, but must be willing to accept authority other than the self. This is the most emotional change that newcomers and experienced members face and the most difficult for all to accept. The first such acceptance of this change usually comes because of what newcomers hear in the meetings.

Generally, Americans have a very low opinion of anyone who is dependent. We believe that people should be able to exploit the abundance of material culture and their own abilities in order to become or remain independent. Americans often express their disgust for individuals who cannot care and provide for themselves. The prevailing, although mistaken, attitude in this country is that everyone is given the same chance to succeed in this land of opportunity and those who cannot take advantage of this benefit of American society fail to live up to the pivotal beliefs and ideals of American cultural ideology. This reluctance to admit dependence on anything outside the self led many members of Alcoholics Anonymous to deny their alcoholism for years and sometimes decades. It has led many more alcoholics who were not able to recover to deny their alcoholism to the death. In the form in which we encounter this critically important, but exaggerated value of self, it appears to be in error. Insofar as we understand the basic structure of human social organization anthropologically, it does not reflect reality. As Radcliffe-Brown stated long ago:

I suggest to you that what makes and keeps a man a social animal is not some herd instinct, but the sense of dependence in the innumerable forms it takes. The process of socialization begins on the first day of an infant's life and it has to learn that it both can and must depend on its parents. From then it has comfort and succor; but it must also submit to their control. What I am really calling the sense of dependence always has these two sides. We can face life and its chances and difficulties with confidence when we know that there are powers, forces and events on which we rely, but we must submit to the control of our conduct by rules which are imposed. The entirely asocial individual would be one who thought that he could be completely independent, relying only on himself, asking for no help and recognizing no duties. (Kuper 1977: 125–126)

This not only is a good summary of the reality that members of Alcoholics Anonymous said they had to submit themselves in order to recover from alcoholism, but it is also an excellent summary of the fundamental error that American cultural ideology presents to individuals in our society. This ideology of autonomy has effectively encouraged the development of an *entire culture* of "asocial" individuals. AA members are encouraged to go to a lot of meetings in order to begin to accept a new reality. Through this new vision of reality they are able to achieve a sense of equality that had eluded them before. It was not the same equality that they had sought before. It was not based on being just as good, just as smart, and just as deserving as the next person, but an equality based on being intrinsically no better than others and one in whom duties and responsibilities took precedence over self-serving actions.

Paradoxically, as AA members achieved sobriety, they were able to achieve many more individual goals consistent with American cultural ideology. As a result of accepting dependence, they were able to regain control over the compulsion to drink and thus over their lives. By giving up the need to keep everything under the control of self, by depending on others, on meetings, and on a higher power, they were able to keep their jobs, pay their bills, and satisfy duties and responsibilities they had to families, friends, and the larger community. In short, they regained self-control, a positive sense of self-esteem, and a functional individual independence.

In summary, the interaction of the meeting demonstrates that Alcoholics Anonymous is indeed a distinctive cultural community. Members share a common world view that is learned, expressed, transmitted, practiced, and perpetuated in the specialized language of a unique speech community. The construction of this shared reality through language fosters a human view of existence on this planet that is very familiar to anthropology and to traditional human social organization. Responsibilities and duties are shared by members and structured by an egalitarian ideology. Human relations are defined by reciprocity, since members cannot keep the "gift" of sobriety unless they give it away. And the demands of material culture in human life cannot be separated from the needs of other human beings or the spiritual essence of existence. The meetings provide the foundation for the shared belief and action of the community, which in turn provide the foundation for healing.

5

Healing in
Alcoholics Anonymous

AA: SPIRITUAL PROGRAM OR RELIGIOUS ORGANIZATION?

The emphasis on the spiritual dimensions of alcoholism and the recovery process is one of the most misunderstood and misinterpreted aspects of the Alcoholics Anonymous program. Many members were unsuccessful in initial attempts to gain sobriety through the AA program because they could not tolerate belief in some "higher power" or the necessity of a "total psychic change." Certainly, there are many more alcohol dependent individuals living in great emotional pain who will never agree to work the program due to this stubborn orientation. This is a tragic fact considering such people's need for a solution to the problem of alcohol dependence.

Members consistently point out that AA is not a religious program, and the traditions of the organization make clear that AA is not, nor wishes to be allied with any "sect, denomination, politics, organization or institution." This is one of the strengths of Alcoholics Anonymous as an organization and a major reason for the success it has enjoyed. While members insist that newcomers must find something outside themselves in which to believe, the emphasis is on "God, *as we understand him.*" Newcomers to AA are encouraged to "find something" that they can consider a higher power. Many members consider the group dynamic as their higher power. This echoes the sentiments of Malinowski in his essay on "The Foundation of Faith and Morals," in which he states, "I, personally, am unable to accept any revealed religion, Christian or not. But even an agnostic has to live by faith—in the case of us pre-war rationalists and liberals, by the faith in humanity and its powers of improvement" (Strenski 1992). Newcomers to AA are told that even atheists and agnostics have to live by faith. It can be faith in the concept of love, grace, acceptance, tolerance, truth, a telephone pole on a city street, or a fence post in the desert, but they are told that they have to believe in something besides their own personal power and gratification.

Alcoholics Anonymous puts great value on the concept of non-interference, and a spiritual way of life and spiritual values are no exception. It does foster gener-osity, charity, love, duty, responsibility, patience, faith, kindness, and hope, but it attaches no concomitant religious requirements to these values. Even Malinowski may have included such values within the scope of "humanity and its powers of improvement." For the most part, the development of the concept of a higher power for use in the battle against alcohol and in daily life is left exclusively to the individual.

A reference to the qualities of God is included in the second tradition, which states, "For our group purpose there is but one ultimate authority, a loving God as He may express Himself in our group conscience. Our leaders are but trusted servants; they do not govern." Most of the references in other AA "conference approved" literature consistently emphasize the loving and benevolent nature of a personal God. Other potential qualities of a higher power are necessarily vague and the organization is very consistent regarding Alcoholics Anonymous as a spiritual rather than a religious program.

The emphasis on the supposed panhuman spiritual qualities of existence on this planet and the reluctance to suggest any specific religious interpretation serves Alcoholics Anonymous and its members in three very important ways. First, those who were enculturated into abusive religious traditions and later rejected the dogma to which they were subjected are encouraged to let go of that kind of concept and develop a new understanding of a higher power. Second, those who are agnostic or atheist are encouraged to believe in something that is tolerable to them rather than that prescribed by narrow religious traditions that they have already thoroughly rejected. And third, those who are members of particular religions are encouraged not to foul the atmosphere of tolerance and personal searching with any specific religious doctrine of their own faith. In this way, more of the individuals who suffer from alcoholism might have a better chance to discover a meaningful, useful, and personal concept of a higher power in order to recover.

However, it is apparent that many outsiders perceive Alcoholics Anonymous as a self-righteous, dogmatic, religious organization. The development of the organi-zation and some individual members have contributed to this misunderstanding. Bill Wilson and Dr. Robert Smith, the co-founders of Alcoholics Anonymous, as well as most other early members of the fellowship, were mostly upper-middle-class Americans who had been enculturated as children into the dominant religious traditions of American culture. Naturally, their conceptions of the spiritual life contained many elements of these specific traditions, which found their way into the 12 steps, the Twelve Traditions, and much of the AA literature.

Traditional biblical translations that always capitalize the word "God" and the pronouns, "He," "Him," and "His" in reference to God itself and the use of the archaic forms such as "Thee," "Thou," and "Thy" are familiar. This familiarity implicates the spirituality of Alcoholics Anonymous as having definite and religious origins. The prayers in the Big Book, which are often recited from memory by various members during the course of discussions, are in this archaic tradition and also lend credence to the objection that AA is a religious program. But the values fostered by the organization are not only familiar to the Judeo-Christian tradition.

They are also familiar to other major, mystical, religious traditions including Islam, Buddhism, and Hinduism. Still, since the majority of Americans are most familiar with their own tradition, they naturally assume that AA is "pushing" some religious program with which they are already thoroughly acquainted. The pious and authoritarian language of many passages in the Big Book can also be a problem for many observers, as well as participating members of the organization. Given the inherent difficulties these factors present to an organization that demands tolerance for a wide variety of beliefs concerning God and that professes to be a spiritual program instead of a religious group, it is amazing that AA has been able to functionally maintain this distinction for 60 years.

In addition to the problems of common values embedded in the language, the use of archaic forms, and the culturally specific religious traditions and concepts with which the founders were familiar, some members are the greatest contributors to this particular misconception. There are many well-intended members who have recovered from alcoholism within Alcoholics Anonymous who nonetheless present themselves, the fellowship, and their conception of God as the only relevant bearers of truth. They can come across as extremely self-righteous. This attitude and the language in which it is expressed is obviously contrary and damaging to the essence of the steps and traditions of AA. No doubt, this drives many alcohol dependent individuals who desperately need help back out the doors of Alcoholics Anonymous. But, in the dynamics of recovery, many other individuals seem to respond to this pious and authoritarian mentality in a positive way. They seem to need to subject themselves to such direction and authority and through this seemingly narrow approach are able to overcome their dependence on alcohol. Here again, this type of individual variation has not precluded the continued development of AA as a spiritual community and has not caused it to develop into a more specifically religious institution.

These problems have not doomed Alcoholics Anonymous to failure, but instead seem to help those who are inclined to believe in this manner. They have not irreparably damaged the organization itself or the hundreds of thousands of members who adamantly practice the principles of anonymity, tolerance, and noninterference. From this study, it is clear that the overwhelming majority of members in AA endeavor to practice the twelfth and final tradition, which states, "Anonymity is the spiritual foundation of all our traditions, ever reminding us to place principles before personalities."

The admonition to place principles before personalities is not an easy one to heed. This is not only difficult in the context of Alcoholics Anonymous, but also in the political sphere, the home, work places, schools, universities, businesses, or religious communities. As human beings, we tend to confuse the exigencies of certain individual personalities and the principles involved with the tasks in which they are engaged. This type of friction is all too common and easily recognized. When critics focus on the failure of a limited number of individuals to live up to their creeds and condemn virtually everyone engaged in similar pursuits, they exhibit chauvinism. Such preconceptions and narrow-minded observations are also a major source of misunderstanding about the spiritual nature of the AA program.

Alcoholics Anonymous is not intended to be a religion, but a spiritual program of living. The philosophy and the ideology of AA are very clear on this matter. The doctrines of this program constitute a definite theology of living that is based in Judeo-Christian traditions, but this theology also incorporates a broad spectrum of modern intellectual and ancient spiritual concerns. It is a modern, generic brand of spirituality and a mystical theology that refuses to identify itself specifically with the traditions from which it has been derived. The reason for this is simple. Alcoholics Anonymous does not want to restrict itself in any matter of belief or faith in order to encourage the individual to be open to the rich potential of the spiritual way of life, regardless of specific cultural or religious formulas, interpretations, or descriptions.

Many members never become active or return to any type of organized religion, and many disparaging remarks about "churches" were observed during the course of this study. But it is obvious that the somewhat amorphous theology of the AA program functions as the basis of ritual practice and a religious institution for many of the members. For many others, who never left or have returned to their own religious traditions, Alcoholics Anonymous serves as a important adjunct to their own personal religious practice. In fact, some members claimed they only began to make progress in their own religious practice after coming to AA. But for most members the 12-step program of AA incorporates the importance of spiritual concerns with the practical morality of everyday life regardless of their personal orientation to religious belief and ritual practice.

PROCEDURES OF HEALING IN ALCOHOLICS ANONYMOUS

Alcoholics Anonymous maintains that recovery is a spiritual healing experience. In order to examine the AA experience in the context of other religious and folk healing practices, it is necessary to maintain an analytic focus that "includes the orientation of the participants within the healing system, their experience of the sacred, the negotiation of possibilities, and the actualization of change" (Csordas 1988: 121). Procedure, process, and outcome are three aspects implicit in such discussions of religious or folk healing practices. These aspects can provide an explicit, systematic focus on which to base analysis. Even though there is a systemic relationship between these three aspects within the healing system and they cannot be seen as altogether discrete, they can function as a framework for understanding the ritual healing practices in Alcoholics Anonymous. By looking closely at these three aspects, we can determine the extent to which the program may be analogous to, and effective as, a folk therapeutic system.

Procedure can be defined as "who does what to whom with respect to medicines administered, prayers recited, objects manipulated, and altered states of consciousness induced or invoked" (Csordas 1988: 121). In this context, the procedure involved when a newcomer arrives is not precisely analogous to the religious and charismatic practices in modern complex societies that he describes, but it is strikingly similar to more traditional systems. In most cases of religious or spiritual healing, the "sick" individual usually presents to a specialist experienced in such practices. The charismatic priest or preacher of modern, complex societies primarily attends to problems of a "spiritual" nature. Economically and socially these specialists may be somewhat set apart from the interactions of ordinary, daily life. However, the shaman or medicine man of more traditional societies is one who specializes in spiritual matters but is also often an ordinary, interactive member of the community. There are also specialized groups in some traditional societies whose members gain status as a community of healers through their own struggle with a particular affliction.

The egalitarian ideology of AA implies that anyone who is working the program can and should assist newcomers in order to help them achieve sobriety. Although established members with longer periods of sobriety are more experienced, many members said that when they first came into AA, it was the relatively new people in the program who seemed to get their attention more readily and to whom it was easier to relate.

Newcomers do not approach AA to receive spiritual healing. When they have decided that they need help, newcomers come to quit drinking. They generally present as "bewildered" and sometimes "terrified" individuals with very little or no real hope for the future. Since AA is supposed to be a "spiritual program," and since everyone claims to suffer from alcoholism, anyone who is sober and working the program can be considered a "specialist" in this regard. Furthermore, considering estimates that indicate that AA successfully reaches only about 5 percent of the total number of alcoholics in the United States, anyone who is successfully working the program of AA and remaining abstinent can objectively be considered a healing specialist.

People who do finally decide to seek help at AA are looking for someone "who knows what they are talking about." Alcoholics Anonymous considers itself a community of healers who are best suited to assist alcoholics by virtue of their common experience. Established members regard this "calling" as necessary to maintain their own sobriety. As members constantly proclaim about the gift of sobriety, "You can't keep it unless you give it away."

Newcomers are attracted by this fact. Most members in this study said they "had tried everything and nothing worked," but in AA they saw many people who had endured similar difficulties and had overcome them. By listening to others' stories, they realized that people in AA knew what they were talking about, but only gradually did they come to perceive the program as one in which spiritual healing was the primary focus. The newcomer is approached by many people with varied lengths of sobriety, greeted, and invited back. I observed that members with longer periods of sobriety usually took it upon themselves to establish communication. Many people with less experience in the program simply do not feel that they have the necessary tools and knowledge to take a leadership role. There are no rules of the organization that define who is best suited to help someone new to AA. Many members in this study emphasized the importance of sharing and helping others almost immediately after beginning to work the program of AA, but as many members said, "You can't give away what you don't have."

A few people with only a month or two of abstinence became very active in trying to help others, but most newcomers require concentration on their own personal struggle. Some are still too wrapped up in themselves to be of much assistance to others. In regard to "who does what to whom," the ideal of Alcoholics Anonymous is that all should and can be of help to the newcomer. This is basically true in practice and was observed during the course of this study. Within a wide range of variation some members provide very little assistance, most feel it is a shared responsibility, and some aggressively extend their help.

Ultimately, it is up to the individual to determine on what level he or she wants to become involved. The ideal is one of non-interference in the affairs of others, so the person who feels that he or she may have a problem with alcohol, can come to the meeting, listen, and decide whether or not to participate in AA. The members of a group have the responsibility to make the individual feel welcome and make certain the newcomer understands that there are people willing to help if they can. Individuals exploring Alcoholics Anonymous can come to the meetings, enjoy the fellowship with others before and after, and make new acquaintances. There is a significant amount of potential interpersonal interaction within the total context of the meeting. While for many people the meeting is the primary way they became involved and continue to affiliate with AA, other people need more assistance to recover and are encouraged to "get a good sponsor."

SPONSORSHIP

Many members are adamant that the newcomer shouldn't try to do it alone. They stress the isolation and loneliness of life before AA, and they point out that the old idea of "I can do it on my own" is a big part of the underlying problem facing the alcoholic when drinking and when in recovery. Besides, as many members said, "The great thing about AA is realizing you don't ever have to be alone again." There are individuals willing to help the newcomer and they are encouraged to make use of them.

In the early development of Alcoholics Anonymous, there were far fewer meetings. In most communities only one meeting a week was held on a rotating basis at the homes of various members. There were also far fewer individuals in the program who could be of assistance. As a result, AA was a very personal program and individuals established close, lasting friendships in sobriety. Today, most metropolitan areas in the United States have dozens and sometimes hundreds of meetings in a single day. The experience of the meeting, usually in a space rented on a permanent basis rather than in someone's home, is relatively less personal. The potential for closeness is still there, but it is not as embedded in the very environment of the meeting itself. Although the ideal behavior regarding newcomers is to make sure that they get help if they want it, AA groups are filled with human beings who are distracted by the necessities of their own lives. Sometimes an individual may not be able to get the help needed within the context of the meetings. Such an individual can be well served by a sponsor.

Sponsors are people who can provide guidance, stability, and encouragement about working the program and the steps of Alcoholics Anonymous. They can't keep anyone from drinking, but they can offer the newcomer a confidant to call on anytime he or she may be experiencing difficulty or confusion that could lead to a drink. Ideally, however, the sponsor is someone who can help the new individual to understand how to "work the steps" and how to apply the principles of AA in daily life. Most of the members at the club have a sponsor on whom they feel they can depend. Dependence on a sponsor is a commitment. Although the relationship of any two individuals involved in sponsorship will be extremely variable and unique, both individuals involved have a specific role. The role of the sponsor is that of a tutor. The role of the person sponsored is that of an obedient student. The student must be prepared to engage in activities that are suggested by the teacher in order to learn to live without alcohol.

Sponsors can be extremely helpful to newcomers in trying to grasp the principles of the program and in working specific steps. Steps four, five, eight, and nine are difficult for most people who affiliate with AA. A great deal of written work is encouraged in order to accomplish steps four and eight. Many people experience these tasks, which are characteristically common to student and academic life, for the first time. For these individuals, writing down all the necessary information is a new experience and many need encouragement. Steps five and nine involve confession and restitution, and the guidance of a sponsor in these matters can be extremely important. A good sponsor can be of enormous help to the individual attempting to recover from alcoholism through the AA program.

Poor sponsors are of little use to the people they sponsor and may even be dangerous. Although AA members try to live by the principles of AA, they are flawed with human frailties. Sometimes they make errors. Many researchers and health care practitioners have severely criticized "sponsors" in Alcoholics Anonymous as untrained and probably incompetent to provide needed counseling. The examples they provide do not inspire confidence (Galanter 1983). However, these examples are not just cause for an indictment of the entire organization and program of Alcoholics Anonymous. From the observations made in this study, poor sponsorship does not appear to be representative of the overall situation.

Some of the more ego-centered and ego-driven individuals in AA are very aggressive and authoritarian. This is in direct contradiction to the principles, values, attitudes, and beliefs expressed in the Twelve Steps and Twelve Traditions, but it happens. Some individuals assume the role of a guru, possibly to the detriment of one newcomer and to the indispensable aid of another. Fortunately, people within AA have begun to address this problem and at least some groups in the local area have started to hold seminars and meetings on sponsorship.

Although there are obvious problems with human beings as sponsors, most members who actively sponsor a number of people devote considerable time and energy in a positive, selfless, and effective way in order to achieve the goal of "helping others." Members said that learning to trust and depend on sponsors also helped them to learn how to trust and depend on their "higher power." Until the newcomer to AA has developed such trust and acceptance, there is no doubt that a sponsor can make the difference between recovery and "going back out." It is difficult to imagine that Alcoholics Anonymous could have grown from 100 individuals to an organization in excess of 1 million members around the world in the span of 60 years without the undying commitment of such people.

MEDICINES

In the early development of Alcoholics Anonymous, it was common and even suggested in the Big Book (AA 1976: 102) that members keep some alcohol available for the purpose of assisting the physically addicted alcoholic. By keeping a half pint of whiskey available, they could help the critically ill alcoholic ease through the symptoms of withdrawal. This resort to alcohol as "medicine" is extremely uncommon today. Such individuals are almost always referred to a "detox" center or public hospital, which are generally available in the urban environment. However, there is a fairly limited range of folk cures that were recommended or provided to some members who suffered from withdrawal symptoms.

Many people talk of being befriended by an AA member when having obvious physical or emotional difficulty in the beginning. From the stories told in meetings, the most common of these suggested remedies is a large glass or pitcher of orange juice and honey. One member said he nursed this concoction throughout his entire first day in an AA club. Some talked of members who took them to get something to eat when they didn't have any money to buy food. One mentioned sitting in a club just drinking "another magic cup of that coffee up there." Many others subscribe to the suggestion in the Big Book that sweets curb the compulsion to drink and should be kept on hand for that purpose. Some people suggest that you "eat some ice cream" whenever you feel like you need a drink. Quite a few people at the club appear to have taken the suggestion of eating ice cream and other sweets seriously.

Although stories of these types of folk cures abound among members of AA, they are minor and for the most part are the only "medicines" that are acceptable to most members. Ironically, any type of drug other than caffeine and nicotine are looked on as mind-altering drugs and are to be avoided. Some newcomers and a few regular members may quietly receive various mood-altering prescription drugs from physicians, but this is not generally acknowledged. Members are continuously warned that medicating one's feelings with any type of drug is "alcoholic thinking." Many members are chain smokers and coffee abusers, but these are not regarded by most AA members as "bad" drugs of the mind-altering category, even though they will readily admit that overindulgence of either one or both is "addictive" behavior and may be hazardous to health. Many people with longer terms of sobriety quit using tobacco for precisely this reason, but the basic attitude is that it's better to use coffee and cigarettes than to drink. Such chemical substitution seems to be a contradiction to the basic principles of the program, but there is considerable sentiment that anything is better than drinking. Many experienced members will tell newcomers to worry about the alcohol (and the "bad" mind-altering drugs) for the first year or so, then tackle other dependencies.

The negative attitude to other drugs is an interesting contrast to subjects in third world populations when they are exposed to modern medicines and how they respond to their availability. These populations seem to want "medicines" not simply because they work, but because they "believe" they work (Van Der Geest and Whyte 1989). AA members claim to feel just the opposite. They tend to reject the belief that there are *any* medicinal or drug substances that can help them and insist that only a "spiritual program" can heal them. This tendency is reflected in an extreme form in a story told in a meeting about a terminally ill cancer patient with over 25 years of sobriety who refused pain-killing medications for agonizing months because he did not "want to throw away all" his sobriety. However, the primary importance of these "cures" is not the physical effect of any medicine. The common significance in all the stories about being helped initially by another recovering alcoholic is that someone else cared about the newcomer's predicament and used his or her energy and resources to help. The act of loving kindness is what impresses the newcomer and begins the healing process. Verbal communication, which leads to the transformation of beliefs and a new program of personal action, is what sustains it, and orange juice and honey, coffee, cigarettes, food, sweets, ice cream, or other substances are like props on a stage.

PRAYER AND MEDITATION

The only specific mention of prayer in the 12 steps is in step 11, which states that "we sought through prayer and meditation to improve our conscious contact with God, as we understood Him, praying only for knowledge of His will for us and the power to carry that out" (AA 1976: 59). Prayer and meditation are important components of most alcoholics' recovery in AA. At every AA group I attended the 12 steps were hanging on the wall and every member spoke of reading those steps the first time they ever went to a meeting. Most newcomers' feelings of ambivalence toward Alcoholics Anonymous and the idea of abstinence are complicated by the words "God" and "prayer" when they first attend a meeting.

If the newcomer has not read the eleventh step on the wall before the first meeting begins, he or she is immediately introduced to the concept of prayer. The opening ritual in the ceremony of the meeting is frequently concluded with a moment of silence followed by the Serenity Prayer. If the newcomer is not presented with the Serenity Prayer at the beginning of the meeting, and if no mention of prayer is made during the meeting, the concluding ritual to the ceremony will invariably be an introduction to the importance of prayer when the chair asks everyone to "stand and close in the usual manner." At this suggestion all in attendance will rise, join hands, and recite the Lord's Prayer. In fact, it is at this point that some newcomers abandon the idea of AA completely and make a hasty exit. Many members expressed the extreme reservations they had about AA when asked to participate for the first time in the concluding prayer. One member, who took seven years in the program to achieve two years of continuous sobriety, recalled his first meeting, "My lawyer told me after my seventh DWI, a felony, that I had to attend AA meetings, or I was going to jail. I didn't like the idea, but I didn't like the idea of jail either, so I went. I sat through the meeting, which was bad enough, but after they got up and joined hands to recite the Lord's Prayer I bolted for the door. It's a good thing nobody got in my way 'cause I was getting out of there." He went to his lawyer the next day and told him there was no way he could tolerate going to those "stupid" meetings, and said that he was going to have to find some other way to keep him out of jail. His lawyer told him that if he didn't start going to meetings before his case came up for judgment, there was no way he could keep him out of jail. He continued to go to meetings to avoid being incarcerated, but for the first couple of years in the program he resented everyone and everything about AA. He didn't believe in God and felt it was useless to engage in prayer. His attitude changed very slowly. Today he considers his belief in God and prayer primary reasons that he can stay sober.

Many individuals at the club expressed their lack of faith in God or the efficacy of prayer when they first entered the program. For most, any belief in a personal and loving God or the value of prayer came gradually. In this respect, discussions of prayer or meditation in the meetings are usually basic and practical. Members extol the value of prayer as an honest surrender to a higher power, a power greater than themselves. Those who feel they don't know how to pray are encouraged to just get down on their knees and say "please" in the morning and "thank you" at night. They are told that asking the unknown and unknowable power outside themselves to help keep them from drinking that day and then thanking that power at night will provide them relief. Agnostics and atheists are encouraged to just try it and see what happens. "After all what have you got to lose?" Many people in this study said that this is the way they began to make progress in the program.

There are two formal prayers in the Big Book that are recommended to those who have no experience with prayer. Both of these are associated with specific steps. The first and most frequently mentioned in meetings is the third-step prayer: "God, I offer myself to thee—to build with me and to do with me as Thou wilt. Relieve me of the bondage of self, that I may better do Thy will. Take away my difficulties, that victory over them may bear witness to those I would help of Thy Power, Thy Love, and Thy Way of Life. May I do Thy will always" (AA 1976: 63). This prayer is suggested to help the individual take step three of the program, which states, "Made a decision to turn our will and our lives over to the care of God, as we understood Him."

The part of this prayer to which was most often referred by speakers and in discussions was "Relieve me of the bondage of self." Having admitted power-lessness over alcohol and the need for help from a higher power, alcoholics in AA try to become ready to submit to something other than personal power. They also prepare to turn their attention to the needs of others and desist from a totally self-centered and self-serving life. More authoritarian members constantly refer to this prayer as a necessary prerequisite to becoming ready to do step four, which calls for "a searching and fearless moral inventory of ourselves." Others doubt that there are any such requirements.

Through the moral inventory (step 4) and admission "to God, to ourselves and another human being the exact nature of our wrongs" (step 5), members said they uncovered some very important things about what was wrong with the way they approached the concept of self and their relations with others. Through this new awareness, they became willing to have such "defects of character" removed (step 6). The next prayer in the Big Book is the seventh-step prayer "My Creator, I am now willing that you should have all of me, good and bad. I pray that you now remove from me every single defect of character which stands in the way of my usefulness to you and my fellows. Grant me strength as I go out from here, to do your bidding, Amen" (AA 1976: 76). In this way AA members, "Humbly asked Him to remove our shortcomings" (step 7).

It is frequently mentioned in meetings that there are really no required prayers. Although most feel that some form of prayer or meditation is necessary to maintain sobriety, specific prayers are only suggestions. Even members with long-term abstinence who maintain agnostic or atheist beliefs feel that some form of meditation or quiet, sober reflection is necessary to stay sober. The importance of some form of prayer is consistent with the idea that alcoholics in AA had reached a point in their lives where they could no longer manage anything and needed help. By accepting this dependence, it is no longer possible to maintain the grandiose illusions and purely self-centered existence of most practicing alcoholics. It facilitates a different view and helps to effect a qualitative change in the perception of self, especially in the context of relations with others.

Members frequently assert that they often go to meetings in an effort to "get outside" themselves. When they cannot attend a meeting, they claim to increasingly rely on prayer and meditation in order to consciously maintain this new perspective concerning the limited power of the self. As one member stated, "All these defects of character are problems inside me that I have to live with. That's just the way it is. Prayer, to try and change it, and meditation to try and recognize it are the only things I have to try and attack this stuff."

MANIPULATED OBJECTS

The primary object that is manipulated to the benefit of the newcomer is the "desire chip." This is a small metallic object, usually a little larger than a quarter, inscribed with various slogans. At meetings of some other groups, a desire chip was offered at the beginning of the meeting, although no one was ever observed accepting one before a meeting. This seemed to be for the benefit of established members since the chip would be offered again at the end of the meeting. Many times someone attending had been inspired to try abstinence. This change of heart at the end demonstrated to regulars and beginners alike that the meetings are important and necessary to recovery.

Some old-timers advised newcomers to "put that chip under your tongue, and when it dissolves you can take a drink." Another recommendation is to carry the chip in the "same place you keep your money so that every time you pull out some change it'll remind you that you're not supposed to be buying anything to drink." Other suggestions included putting a hole in it in order to carry it on a key ring. And the most magical suggestion of all was "just rub it when you have a compulsion to take a drink." When people relapse they are encouraged to "trade in a wet one for a dry one." These are some of the magical qualities that may be ascribed to the chip.

Chips are also offered to people celebrating various "increments of sobriety." Chips of one, two, three, six, and nine months are given to new members as they reach these goals. These are relatively inexpensive chips, but the more elaborate and permanent ones begin with one year. Every year, when a member celebrates another "birthday," he or she receives another chip that indicates the number of years of continuous sobriety achieved. Occasionally, some members were observed extending an old chip that had served them as a "charm" to a newcomer, but most people have a fond reverence for the chips they have received in the course of abstinence and guardedly view them as magical if not sacred objects.

The only other object that is revered is the Big Book of Alcoholics Anonymous. Although the manipulation of this book is qualitatively different from the chips, it is nonetheless considered to be of vital material importance to the process of recovery in AA. Newcomers are encouraged to buy one or sometimes a member will make a gift of the book. Many hardcore members maintain that all the wisdom one needs to recover from alcoholism can be read in its pages.

ALTERED STATES OF CONSCIOUSNESS

An altered state of consciousness is immediately encouraged in Alcoholics Anonymous. Ironically, the first altered state of consciousness that is suggested is one of sobriety, and newcomers are told that it can be induced by *NOT DRINKING*. This does not simply signify the avoidance of intoxicated states. Members suggest that years of resorting to alcohol had seriously affected not only the way they reasoned when drinking, but had affected their reasoning process even when not drinking. They claimed that even the memory of life itself had been affected.

Newcomers are encouraged not to drink so that they can honestly begin to remember the things that have happened in the past and the role of alcohol in those experiences. They suggested that the longer one stayed sober, the more one could remember. They said that with enough time away from intoxication, a totally new perspective on life would begin to emerge. This is not only a new perception of the present and the future, but the altered state of sobriety catalyzes a new, more accurate and adequate framework for knowledge and understanding of past experience.

Alcoholics in this study generally agreed that it was not only being intoxicated that led to their problems, but their entire way of thinking and their conception of their place in the world was flawed. They claimed that this world view contributed significantly to the development of their alcoholism. As they turned more and more to alcohol to "medicate their feelings," they turned more and more away from responsibility for their own actions. Bad things that happened to them were always somebody else's fault. They harbored deep resentment for the least intrusion into their own sense of the meaning of life. They wanted what they wanted. Any obstacle to that was not tolerated. Nobody was going to tell them what to do. They didn't respond well to authority and kept telling themselves, "Alcohol's not the problem. I can handle drinking if I could just get this other stuff in my life straightened out."

They drank when they got angry, which they were with increasing frequency.

They drank because they felt inferior, and with increasing loss of control over drinking and behavior they suffered from even lower self-esteem. They drank because they felt superior and alcohol increasingly provided them with the only illusion that they were better than everyone else. They drank because the dog was sick. They drank because the dog was not sick. They drank because their spouse was angry. They drank because they were sad. They drank because they were happy. In the end they drank, "Over everything, good or bad."

Recovery in AA is not only dedicated to abstinence, but to a "total psychic change." However, members maintained that before any changes whatsoever can occur, the alcohol must go. The beginning of abstinence initiates a transformation in reasoning due to an altered state of consciousness induced by not drinking. If newcomers begin to accept the program and total abstinence as an answer to their problems, then they are encouraged to pray and meditate in order to achieve a different conscious awareness. However, the single most important thing for the newcomer or the established member is to not use alcohol. Members said that without this altered state of consciousness one can never hope to really get better. They maintained that as long as the alcoholic's belief in "old ideas" persists, he or she cannot recover.

THE PROCESS OF HEALING IN ALCOHOLICS ANONYMOUS

Whether Alcoholics Anonymous or other folk healing practices are the focus of research, such procedures are relatively straightforward and obvious to the dedicated observer. However, "What is needed at this stage of development of a theory of healing is specification of how therapeutic process effects transformation in existential states. An approach grounded in participants' own experience and perceptions of change may arrive at a more pragmatic conceptualization of healing as a cultural process" (Csordas 1988: 128). The procedures of healing that are experienced by the AA member have little or no utility in effecting recovery in and of themselves. Having a sponsor will not insure abstinence and sobriety. Accepting a desire chip or reading the Big Book will not keep one from drinking. Prayer without faith is merely a scream in the dark. And not drinking will only lead to greater pain and suffering if unaccompanied by actual changes in thinking and behavior. Members maintain that only through a fundamental change in the way the individual perceives the world and the way in which one responds to this new perception can the alcoholic truly recover from alcoholism. Alcoholics Anonymous does not advocate a magical cure, but a continuing and gradual *process* by which the individual alcoholic is transformed. This process is the essential mechanism of healing, which is practiced throught the 12-step program. In order to examine this process, it is necessary to describe the "participants' experience with respect to encounters of the sacred, episodes of insight, or changes in thought, emotion, attitude, meaning, and behavior" (Csordas 1988: 121).

The attempt to conceptually describe these encounters, insights, and changes as a process must take place in the context of the experience of participating AA members. Through actual, intensive participation in the 12-step program of

Alcoholics Anonymous, the alcohol dependent individual is changed and healed. By looking at this process we can reveal how such change begins to occur. Very few individuals claimed to have had vivid, spiritually meaningful visions or other extraordinary experiences concerning the sacred, although it does occur. More often, newcomers are told not to expect a full-blown, "burning bush" experience and to resolve themselves to a long, educational experience of the sacred in their lives.

In order to participate in the program of Alcoholics Anonymous, "the only requirement is a desire to stop drinking." The "qualifications" of different individuals are extremely variable. Most members had to overcome the apparent differences between others in the program and the perception of their own experience in order to begin working the program. Everyone's story is personal. Almost all the subjects of this study initially saw this variability as sufficient evidence to reject the program as a description of their problem or as a possible solution. They sought to focus on the differences in other people's stories rather than the similarities. In general, the problems associated with the use of alcohol can be very similar. However, when a person relates his or her personal experience, it is by definition unique to that particular individual. Many people used the differences they perceived in their own experiences to separate themselves from the "disgusting alcoholics" at an AA meeting. Denial is systemic and the enormous resilience of the individual's denial system readily facilitates such distinctions. Many members said that although they knew they had a problem with alcohol, they simply could not admit that they were alcoholic. When initially exposed to the concepts of AA, they sought to distance themselves from "those people in AA." They looked for the slightest differences between their experience and the experience of those in AA. They used such variation as an excuse to shroud themselves in denial. Members said that this is the first attitude or belief that must change in order to recover.

All members recalled various incidents, which in retrospect seem to have been spiritual experiences or at least enabled them to have critical insight concerning the problem of alcohol in their lives, and the possibility of a solution. For example, many individuals in AA were daily drinkers who could not get out of bed without a drink. My own initial reaction to such stories was typical. When I got my second DWI in 1987, I knew I had a problem with alcohol. The probation department assigned me to one AA meeting a week as a condition of my probation and also made me attend the DWI School. I was glad to attend, since I knew I had an alcohol problem. When I went to the DWI School, they gave us a diagnostic test. It contained 19 questions that were supposed to tell whether or not you were an alcoholic. A "yes" answer to three or four questions indicated you probably had a drinking problem, and if you answered yes to more than that, you were definitely an alcoholic. At that point in my life I had decided to be honest because things were pretty much out of control. I answered the questions truthfully and got 16 out of 19—yes. They interviewed me and asked me if I realized that I was probably an alcoholic and I agreed with them at that time, but I guess I was just playing the game with the legal system. I hadn't been to my first AA meeting when I took the test. There were only three questions I had answered "no." I didn't drink alone, I didn't drink everyday, and I didn't ever take a drink in the morning to ease a hangover. Well, when I went to AA, all these alcoholics kept talking about not being able to start the day without a drink, drinking everyday, and drinking by themselves because they didn't have any friends left, so I said, "I'm not like these idiots, I'm not an alcoholic." I went to a meeting every week for two years, but I never accepted abstinence as a solution. I went to learn how to control my drinking. For those two years I was fairly successful. I didn't get arrested and I didn't really hurt anyone physically, so when I got off probation I stopped going to AA. For the next two years everything went completely out of control. In the end I was drinking everyday, drinking in the morning when I didn't have to work, and pretty much a solitary drinker.

This type of story is very common among AA members. Although each individual will have personalized variations, the general theme is one of losing control, first over drinking, then over other aspects of everyday existence. This is followed by an awareness that a problem exists, but a continuing denial that the problem is "alcoholism." Finally, the ego structure that displaces, minimizes, and rationalizes the behavior collapses due to the massive accumulation of empirical evidence gathered over an extended period of time by the individual (Brown 1985). Once this collapse takes place and the individual "hits bottom," the process of change has begun and it is possible to recover. New insight and conceptual awareness are the products of the process and absolutely necessary to recovery. AA members are initially assaulted with the necessity of two vital changes. They are told that they should conceive of the problem of alcoholism as an affliction of the mind, body, and spirit rather than an intrinsic, personal, moral weakness (step 1). And they are told that it is absolutely necessary that they come "to believe that only a power greater than ourselves can restore us to sanity" (step 2). AA maintains that these two concepts are a part of "letting go of the old ideas" and critical to the process of recovery.

MORAL WEAKNESS OR DISEASE

The first "old idea" that Alcoholics Anonymous seeks to help the newcomer dispel is that alcoholism is a defect of moral character. AA was founded on two principles—that alcoholism was a disease of the body, mind, and spirit and that it could be overcome only by conversion and transformation of belief. Some members often refer to the "fact" that "I've got a disease" or "I'm allergic to alcohol." Some simply accept that they cannot use alcohol due to some pathological condition from which they suffer. At the other end of the spectrum, some members have a difficult time believing that alcoholics are "made" by the accident of genetics and birth. Their experience has led them to believe that it is a sickness that can develop in anyone who works at it hard enough.

Harris (1989) notes that hospital patients in American culture need the "doctor's opinion," just as presented in the first chapter of the Big Book (AA 1976), as an explanation of the mechanical way in which the world works, but when faced with injury and illness, they also need to be able to interpret the event morally. Alcoholics Anonymous presents individuals with a possible pathological explanation and a moral interpretation. In this way AA takes into account the biological, psychological, social, and spiritual causes of alcoholism. Harris adds that "people with severe conditions tend to probe deeper into moral meaning" (1989: 15). In her study of five patients hospitalized with severe conditions, she found that all expressed a belief that God or some power greater than themselves was an active part in their condition, whether it be a negative or positive influence. It is interesting that AA members seem to be people who have suffered severely due to their practice of alcoholism. It is also extremely interesting that, coincidentally, two of the five patients in her study were hospitalized due to alcohol.

Estroff and colleagues, in describing the self-labelling behavior of psychiatric patients, suggest "that individuals' understandings of their problems, more than formal designations like a psychiatric diagnosis, have a strong influence on their views of themselves in relation to mental illness. Self-labelling . . . is clearly influenced by many factors which are not clinical, but contextual, experiential, and sociocultural" (1991: 361).

The belief in a higher power and the type of self-labelling, self-justification, and identity talk revealed in these two studies have important implications for the study of AA. It is clear that AA members use the identification of themselves as "alcoholic" to recognize their inclusion in a category that may have been diagnosed by health professionals or, more commonly, was based on their own experience. In this case, while they accept inclusion in this abnormal class of individuals, they can also normalize their condition if they have accepted the disease concept of alcoholism to some extent. They further normalize their behavior with repeated assertions that all alcoholics are "sick." Given the fact that the class of alcoholics in the United States is quite large, they can normalize their own illness even further. This can be quite useful in ridding oneself of excessive guilt and shame relevant to past actions. The whole disease concept is one that many members find to be comforting. Once they have accepted that alcoholism is a disease or some unknown pathological proclivity, they have a rational explanation for their inability to successfully drink alcohol. It is out of their control. Since they have no control and because they are ill, they are able to accept much more readily the proposition that they are powerless over alcohol.

Some individuals in AA may have a tendency to absolve themselves of the responsibility for past actions through a destructive manipulation of the disease concept of alcoholism, but the AA member who expects others to automatically understand and forgive past transgressions because the member was afflicted with this condition and failed to realize it is deluding himself or herself. That member's recovery rests on a shaky foundation. Most members observed in this study were not interested in the disease concept as an excuse for their behavior. Members continually stressed the necessity of taking responsibility for one's own actions. The disease concept provides a focus that can be utilized by the newcomer to better understand the mysterious and complicated nature of alcohol dependency. One thing is certain; the subjects of this study do not believe that inclusion in a normalized, though deviant and diseased, group will heal them. They believe that once individuals have begun the process of healing through the insight that they are powerless over alcohol (step 1), they must continue to open themselves to the process of change through acceptance that only "a power greater than ourselves can restore us to sanity" (step 2).

THE CONCEPT OF GOD

A subdued tone can come over a group when a discussion centers specifically on the concept of God. This is hardly surprising since people have great difficulty explaining exactly who or what God is. For atheists "God" is simply a myth. For most AA members the inability to explain God is simply an extension of the mystery concerning God's existence with which they have been faced throughout their lives. Many members claim they held atheist or agnostic beliefs when they came to Alcoholics Anonymous. Many members came to the program with a vengeful and dysfunctional concept of God. Some came to the program with a belief in God, but very little faith in the practicality of such belief.

Members said that it is not surprising that practicing alcoholics had little use for God. Many said they had assumed the role of God in their lives and had no need for any concept of a higher power. The denial of God's existence functioned in defense of the denial of their alcoholism. If there was no higher power than themselves, then they didn't have to concern themselves with anyone else's welfare. They didn't need to quit drinking because it was not a problem. This attitude also fostered a sense of the hopelessness and meaninglessness of life. Many individuals claimed that they were atheists when they entered the AA program. The concept of God was frequently the reason they had rejected repeatedly the idea of AA before finally giving up. Most of these individuals ultimately accepted a belief in a "God of *my* understanding." This is probably the most important reason for the success of Alcoholics Anonymous over almost six decades. Even though the newcomer had no belief in God on arrival he or she was told, "You may be suffering from an illness which only a spiritual experience will conquer" (AA 1976: 44). This conclusion is most often the reason for a newcomer, in a meeting for the first time, to leave determined never to return because "to one who is an atheist or agnostic such an experience seems impossible" (AA 1976: 44). However, the reason they ultimately took it into consideration is that they had put themselves in a position "to be doomed to alcoholic death or live on a spiritual basis" (AA 1976: 44). This was their last hope. No alcoholic in this study really wanted to quit drinking, or wanted to change the way he or she thought, but they were at the end of the rope. Nothing else had worked. They had tried everything and they were out of options. They were told by others that "you don't have to believe in anyone else's God, just find something that you can understand." AA maintains that the alcoholic attempting to recover needs a higher power—something on which one can truly depend and an acceptance of that dependence. Many members are vehemently anti-religious and many of them remain so. Atheists, agnostics, and some of those who were brought up in abusive religious traditions that focused on sin, penance, crime, punishment, and an eventual trip to hell are among the anti-religious in AA. They felt that the God of wrath who had been taught to them as children in these traditions would never help them. Many members had been enculturated into loving religious traditions, but as adults they later accepted the "superior" value of rationalism and science that we highly regard in American culture. They came to feel that a belief in God and a belief in science and rationalism were mutually exclusive. They decided that belief in God was for the stupid, the ignorant, and the uneducated. As one woman said, "In the crowd I hung around with, belief in God was not very smart. I don't know why. But everybody thought it was much more intelligent to not believe."

Most members really believed that to be dependent was to be weak. They felt that others they knew valued self-sufficiency above all and they wanted the acceptance of those others. At the same time, they were incredibly dependent on others in their drinking life. The grandiosity of the alcoholic thinking that controlled their perceptions of the world around them had to be replaced with something else. Levin (1987) suggests that anyone referred to AA be warned, "Do not let any prejudice you may have against spiritual terms deter you from honestly asking yourself what they mean to you." This openness has led many to the acceptance of many beliefs that seemed impossible before. God is one of the impossible things that changes for most people who work the steps of Alcoholics Anonymous. AA members stressed that the alcoholic must accept some higher power in order to begin the process of recovery. For many newcomers and some who have been in the program for a long time, the group is considered the higher power. They began to believe, as one member said and many have repeated, "because I see how God has been working in my life through the people in this program." Members said that tolerance developed for the belief that there may be spiritual principles that are more important than the material reality of the world.

Members stressed that each individual must have a conception of a higher power, which must have *relevance to reality*. This synthesis of spirituality and practical morality is one of the great strengths of Alcoholics Anonymous. God must be relevant to everyday life. Members claimed that in the beginning, they did not want to accept that God is real, but they decided that they needed the help so badly, they were willing to try to believe. As one member said, "Everybody in this program would be better off if they would just suspend all disbelief, and for five minutes each day accept everything in the first three steps as true."

The bottom line in the Big Book and among members is that the acceptance of our limitations as human beings, the wisdom to recognize that we do not have all the answers, that we do not have sufficient information, and that we do not own the truth to categorically state that there is no God, is the beginning. The rest is a mystery. They don't claim to know how it works. People in meetings just keep saying that it does. They believe that there is some power of existence in the universe that we are not able to fully comprehend or explain, and they believe that as human beings we are all a part of that existence.

When a newcomer or a member makes a decision to consider the possibility and to "turn our lives and our will over to the care of God, as we understand Him" (step

3), then he or she is able to continue with the other steps of the program. As members recover, they no longer are in a position to argue whether or not it exists. Most said that "but for the Grace of God," they would be dead or miserable. Instead they became well and have experienced a mysterious healing power that they could call anything they wanted, but which most choose to call God.

6

Alcoholic Thinking

"Alcoholic thinking" refers to the set of beliefs upon which practicing alcoholics base their behavior. Alcoholic thinking led them to believe that the use of alcohol was at first desirable, then necessary, and eventually an inevitable part of their existence. Members of Alcoholics Anonymous constantly talked about "alcoholic thinking." They attributed many errors of the past and the present to such a mental process. Alcoholic thinking was often blamed for failure to make proper progress in the program and even after significant periods of sobriety, it was the primary affliction for which many claimed to remain active participants in AA. Almost all asserted that it was the underlying culprit in their alcoholism. For most, alcoholic thinking supported for years the illusion of a rational dependence on alcohol.

One evening, at a 6:30 discussion meeting at the club, one of the members was going around the room extending an invitation to chair the meeting to various members, all of whom begged off. The last one sitting near me pointed his thumb over his shoulder in a deprecating gesture to me and said, "There's a guy right back here that needs to chair a meeting." I accepted the preamble and called the meeting to order by beginning to read. At the club, anyone may chair a meeting or read "How It Works." It is customary for more established members to involve everyone in this part of the ceremony. Most people agree to such formal participation in the meetings and feel more involved as a result of this activity. Such action lends itself to changing the initial feeling that one is attending "their" meetings, and helps to transform the new member's identity, as these gatherings become "our" meetings. This attitude is frequently cited by members as a perspective that is necessary in order to recover. Newcomers need to feel that they belong in a group of alcoholics. Some members are not particularly verbal, but with a few exceptions, who chairs the meeting and reads "How It Works" or the Twelve Traditions is the result of a loosely rotating basis that reflects the highly egalitarian nature of the fellowship. At some of the larger and more organized groups in the local area, these roles are more formally constituted and prearranged. However, at the club most of the meetings are discussions and this spontaneity is the norm.

After reading the preamble, "How It Works," and the Twelve Traditions, I omitted the Serenity Prayer and began the discussion, for which I was later chastised by one of the members in attendance. Different groups are autonomous in how they want to structure the meeting. Although I know of no formal policy to pause for "a moment of silence followed by the Serenity Prayer," it is generally done by most people who chair a meeting at the club. It is definitely a traditional practice of this particular group, and it was a grave omission in the opinion of some. As I was told after the meeting, "Well, it may not be a rule, but an opening prayer certainly never hurts." Having heard repeated references to "alcoholic thinking" in the meetings, I suggested that we talk about how not drinking and the AA program had helped them to change this alcoholic thinking. I asked them to compare alcoholic thinking with the way they think now.

The first woman to respond said that her thinking had changed a lot since she came into the program, "this last time," but her thinking was still all messed up. She really hoped that if she kept working the program and not drinking that eventually, it would improve. She said no progress could be made without removing the alcohol. She still had emotional problems that she needed to address, and changes in her thinking that needed to occur. Her response reflects a very common sentiment. Many people are aware that they suffer from emotional problems, but all expressed the belief that alcohol had to be eliminated before progress could be achieved. This is the *focus* of Alcoholics Anonymous. The next man said that although there were some dramatic improvements in his thinking due to sobriety, he felt that it was a long, slow process to change his thinking. "My best thinking is what got me to the program of Alcoholics Anonymous." This is a favorite slogan whenever the topic of thinking comes up and is often used to illustrate the necessity of depending on a higher power.

In response to the suggested topic, these first two members had focused on the concept of change within the program of Alcoholics Anonymous. This is also a common topic for meetings. Change is probably the most fundamental concept in the AA recovery process. It is often mentioned that in order to recover from alcoholism one has to undergo "a total psychic change." Although some people had sudden, dramatic experiences, most had an educational conversion. The gradual nature of this process is often frustrating to the AA member. All members said that before any changes could begin to have a measurable effect on their lives, they had to eliminate alcohol and work the steps. By "practicing these principles in all our affairs" there is hope to effect this change in thinking. Members agreed that they "had to get rid of alcoholic thinking."

As the discussion began to move around the room, the central theme of change began to interact with most of the pivotal concepts that are frequently addressed and that are often topics for entire meetings. "Alcoholic thinking" is the underlying system of beliefs with which the individual is armed and that form the "basis of a commitment to action" (Goodenough 1990: 609, Kearney 1975). The phrase "alcoholic thinking" implies that the individual's belief system has been significantly and predictably changed and impaired as a side effect of alcohol use.

An examination of important concepts that are repeatedly suggested as topics for discussion demonstrates how people perceive the "old ideas" they held during their active "drinking careers." Through the discussion of these concepts after they have begun to change their thinking, it is possible to show the intellectual, emotional, and spiritual basis of the recovery process in the AA program.

The manner in which members refer to alcoholic thinking clearly indicates that it is not simply intoxicated thinking, but the *entire system of values and beliefs on which they based their attitudes and behavior* that led them to drink in the first place, led them to become alcohol dependent, and precluded any solution, in most cases for many years. In short, alcoholic thinking is the way that their interpretation of values and beliefs they acquired as members of American culture conflicted with and confused the reality of existence. Such a process implies that one may not have to be an alcoholic to think like one. Other individuals attempt to deal with these conflicting values and the resulting confusion through other addictive behaviors. This is probably why the 12-step program has been successfully adapted to many other behavioral disorders.

The process of change to which AA members submit themselves initiates and sustains many episodes of insight and substantial changes in thoughts, emotions, and attitudes concerning meaning and behavior. These spiritual encounters, insights, and changes are repeatedly presented by individual members through the dynamic interaction of the meeting. And it is through this redundancy that most AA members gradually and increasingly understand of the recovery process in their own lives. Members said that they had to hear the same things over and over again before they finally came to have some real meaning. It is through such repetition and repeated exposure to the principles of the program that they learn how to transform their thinking and their lives until they have outgrown the necessity of taking a drink to cope with daily life.

Examining a number of these topics repeatedly used in discussions will not exhaustively cover all the concerns of the AA group, but it will represent the most pivotal and vital concepts necessary to recovery. Although many discussions focus on a particular step, other discussions center specifically on one of the important concepts or values promoted as a way to *actualize the steps* in daily life. Usually, a tapestry of ideas is woven by the various members in attendance as they personally respond to the suggested issue. This is the basic healing action of the AA program. As members "share their experience, strength, and hope," they reveal the process of healing.

Most established members would agree that the concepts, values, and meanings embedded in the discussion of topics cannot be discretely separated when discussing the process of alcohol use, dependence, and recovery. But it is possible to make some general distinctions about these concepts, values, and meanings in the context of working the program and different stages of recovery. Recognition of the problem and its underlying causes is the first stage of the process. Acceptance of the program of AA as a solution follows such recognition. And the maintenance of sobriety succeeds as a result of the ongoing personal and spiritual growth nurtured through daily action by the 12-step program of Alcoholics Anonymous.

THE PROBLEM

People Pleasers

Discussions in meetings often focused on the way in which humans beings are influenced by others. Many spoke of a yearning to belong and earn the acceptance of others. They spoke of the things they had been willing to do to please other people in their lives. Most members said that to some extent they started drinking to be part of the crowd. Alcohol intoxication enabled them to discard the fear of others, shyness, and anxiety. It helped them to become one of the gang. The "social lubricant" of alcohol was extremely helpful in this regard. It took away feelings of inadequacy and effectively substituted feelings of power, confidence, and influence.

The need to please others and the perceived failure to do so were often cited as among the main reasons they drank. Generally, these members exhibited obvious anxiety concerning the opinion of other people, which really emphasizes our social needs as human beings. In America, the value that we place on individuality and independence is enormous. But, no matter how much stock we put in these concepts, we cannot avoid the social imperatives of our human nature. We are social animals with social needs and these cannot be escaped.

Many members said that initial contact with the AA program was not successful because they were not doing it for themselves, but to please a spouse, a parent, an employer, or some significant other human being. They went initially to make someone else happy, not because they were committed to the idea that they had to change their lives or even stop drinking. The social exigencies of human existence had a profound effect on members' initial enculturation into the drinking culture, had a substantial effect on the specific patterns that developed in the course of their drinking, and also played a vital part in their decision to discontinue the use of alcohol. But this concern for others resurfaced in recovery in a different context. They said that concern for others is what keeps them "in the solution" and sober, instead of in the "problem" and hopeless.

Hopelessness

Some members first came to AA without any sense of hopelessness or "impending doom," but usually they did not work the program or accept any of its main tenets. They attended meetings with a hidden agenda. Some went because their spouse insisted that they do something about their drinking. Some were required to attend meetings as a condition of probation for an alcohol related offense, such as DWI. These individuals attended AA under duress and more often than not did not accept abstinence as an answer to their problems. Even if they knew they had a problem with alcohol, they minimized and rationalized in order to maintain denial and delay identification as an alcoholic.

Most members said that this attitude was their initial response to the program of AA. Almost all said that they rejected the program, not only as a solution, but usually rejected the very definition of the problem. Yet, all members said that by the time they began to actually "work the program," they had nowhere else to turn. Their lives were a mess and they had no idea what to do. They felt like they "didn't know how to live with alcohol" and they "couldn't imagine life without alcohol." Many said that they wanted to die but didn't have the courage to commit suicide.

Virtually all members repeatedly tried to quit drinking on their own, but no one claimed that he or she was ultimately successful. Eventually, they always returned to drinking and usually with progressively more disastrous results. Most readily claimed that they were "insane." Many had tried treatment centers, other types of intervention, and "cures." They had no success maintaining their abstinence. One member said that he had been homeless for three years and had developed the use of a circuit of treatment centers in various cities around the country. Most had severe problems with family, employers, and other people. Many had repeated problems with the legal system. On entering the AA program many said that they had no real hope that AA would help either, but that they were at the end of the line and didn't know what else to do. This incredible feeling of hopelessness made them ready to try anything. They had "hit bottom."

The person most likely to accept the AA program as a definition of the problem and as a possible solution appears to be the person who has attended AA before, has finally run out of hope, and is tired of suffering. They tried AA, not because they believed it would help them, but because they felt that they had exhausted all the possible alternatives, none of the alternatives had worked, and the pain had become unbearable. They became more and more aware that there was a problem. They regretted the losses they had sustained in life. Some lost jobs and the financial basis for life no longer existed. Some lost spouses and entire families. Most lost virtually all productive social relationships. All lost any type of healthy self-image. They had been stripped of their self-respect. There was none left. The vast complex of egocentric rationalization and minimization that they had constructed to explain their behavior and maintain their ego had collapsed, and as they began to participate in Alcoholics Anonymous they felt utterly hopeless. They had empirically verified the fact that they were powerless over alcohol.

Powerlessness

The first step that the alcoholic must take in order to recover, according to the AA program, is to admit, "We were powerless over alcohol and that our lives had become unmanageable" (step 1). Repeatedly, members said that "this is the one step we have to take one hundred percent." They said that if anyone harbored the smallest doubt that step one was an accurate reflection of his or her relationship to alcohol, then that person would have difficulty maintaining abstinence as a way of life because "the dream of every alcoholic is to be able to drink like normal people."

Many people initially came to AA in a hopeless and bewildered state. They were more than willing to admit their powerlessness at that point. However, as they achieved some small measure of sobriety and began to think that control over life was returning, they started to think that they had learned enough. "This time it'll be different," they predicted. This is never the case with the true alcoholic. Although they may try to return to "controlled drinking," failure inevitably results. Most members tried to return to controlled drinking after periods of abstinence in AA, and they were invariably forced to return to the program or continue to suffer the consequences of their drinking. Some members referred to this behavior as "a little research and development."

Some who were coerced into the program by family, employers, or the legal system were willing to admit that they were powerless over alcohol, but they thought that they were managing their lives quite well. The denial syndrome tended to remain active if they had a job, had never been dismissed due to alcohol use, did not miss too much work because of hangovers, paid their bills, and felt in control of most aspects of daily life. Even if all of these things were not true, they may have convinced themselves that they were true, especially if their situation seemed to be fairly tolerable. One member related the following story:

When I first came to AA because of the legal system, I realized that I was powerless when I drank too much, but I felt that it was the other disappointments in my life that caused me to drink too much. I was willing to consider that I was powerless over alcohol, but I was managing my life just fine except for the cops who kept stopping me and throwing me in jail. I had a good job, didn't feel that alcohol had ever interfered with my work, and had a good social life and a nice place to live. I guess that's why I rejected AA the first time around. Five years later when I went to AA to get some help my life was unmanageable, and after I had been sober for a while I realized that alcohol had destroyed most of my relationships with women, with the people I worked for, and with my family. It had caused incredible financial difficulties. Sober reflection made me realize that even though it wasn't nearly as bad as it was going to get, it was pretty bad back then. I just wasn't ready to admit that alcohol was the problem.

All members who actively work the program readily admit that they are powerless over alcohol. Stories they tell in the meetings about their behavior while under the influence would not give anyone any reason to doubt this assertion. They refer to the loss of control as an absolute fact that they have empirically validated through their experience. Members said "Not only am I powerless over alcohol, but I'm powerless over people, places, and things." Manipulative behavior and the compulsion to control everything around them are considered by many members to be one of the big reasons that they drank. They wanted others to do what they wanted them to do, and when these attempts at control were frustrated, they drank to alleviate the discomfort. They felt that they had to be in control of themselves and everyone around them. They could not accept things as being out of their own personal control. Many expressed the belief that if "other people would just act right," they wouldn't have so many problems. Most members said that as long as they tried to control other people and events, they experienced frustration, anxiety, difficulty, and fear that all mitigated against recovery.

Fear

Members agreed that fear was one of the great contributors to their dependence on alcohol. Most said that when they first began to drink, alcohol was very effective in helping them to deal with their fears. If they were afraid to speak their mind in a group of people, alcohol splendidly loosened their tongues. When afraid that they were "apart" from others, alcohol made them feel togetherness and community. When they felt ugly, alcohol made them feel sexy. When they felt inadequate, alcohol gave them confidence. When they felt weak, alcohol gave them strength and power. Alcohol was the elixir of life and the greatest killer of fears that they had in their behavioral arsenal. Although it took away the fear, this effect was temporary. When the fear returned in even greater fury, it became a habit to conquer the feeling by consuming alcohol.

Eventually "alcohol quit working," and fears became "terrors." Although many alcoholics kept saying, "I'm not afraid of anything," like the lion in *The Wizard of Oz*, they were thoroughly frightened. The lack of control and the unmanageability of life were terrifying. Most AA members were in precisely such a terrorized state when they came to the program. After they began to recover, they had to discover some way to deal with fear. If they did not, they had little hope of remaining sober or even abstinent.

As people became abstinent and began dealing with their fears on a sober basis, they invariably began to feel that their greatest fears "had been of losing something" they didn't have anyway. As one member put it, "After I had been sober about ten days I thought, I've got a serious problem. What am I going to do for fun?" This thought came from a man who entered AA as a hopeless skid row bum. He referred to even the existence of such a thought as "insanity." As a homeless, physically addicted drunk he had not been having any "fun" whatsoever, yet the thought persisted. He said that this exemplified alcoholic thinking and illustrated the importance of maintaining abstinence "long enough to begin to change my thinking." Irrational fears, accompanied by the attendant anxiety that they caused, constituted an important reason why members in this study became alcohol dependent. They are also one of the biggest obstacles to sobriety. Many members said that they did not know how to handle such fears, so they became angry.

Anger

One way in which the typical alcoholic in this study responded to fear in life was through anger. The specific type of anger is as variable as are the types of alcoholics in the program. Some harbored quiet, seething, gestating anger, which they kept to themselves. Many members, particularly, but not exclusively males, developed anger to an especially destructive degree. As one said, "I acted out of anger my entire life, and when I first came to AA I thought it was my right to be angry with anyone who didn't live up to my selfish expectations." Many expressed the relish with which they nourished their anger and said that it was all a part of feeling "ten feet tall and bulletproof."

Meetings are full of tragic stories involving the development and use of anger as an interpersonal tool. Some said that they vented their anger on loved ones and complete and total strangers alike. When they had an object for their anger, they could displace the feelings of inadequacy and impotence that formed their deepest beliefs about themselves. Many said that they could not function without alcohol. It became the most important tool they had to maintain their denial of responsibility for their troubles. It helped them to maintain their anger. Many times they acted out of anger in order to regulate the environment, and members said it led to incredible stupidity. Whether or not the anger is acted on appears to be irrelevant. As the individual began to rationally depend on anger to support the ego structure, anger was internalized and bred persistent resentments.

Resentments

Resentments are identified by the Big Book of Alcoholics Anonymous and by most members as the number one enemy of the alcoholic. AA maintains that as long as the individual holds onto resentments toward other people, institutions, or any other animate or inanimate object, there is the danger of drinking oneself to death. They suggest that only through a constructive approach, that allows the alcoholic to "let go" of resentments can any solution can be found. They cannot "hold on" to these resentments because the anxiety that they invariably produce and the rationalizations that they usually produce enable alcoholics to blame someone or something else for their troubles. This is the very reason for the fourth step, which states that "we made a searching and fearless moral inventory of ourselves."

In order to make an inventory, it is suggested that the individual make a list of the resentments from which they currently suffer, or have held in the past. From this list of resentments, members said they made an effort to discover why they had these resentments. They listed the action that or person who had caused the resentment to develop. They identified how situations had caused them fear or shame, how their self-esteem or sex lives had suffered, and the financial difficulties or family problems that had arisen in their interactions with others. These specific ways in which the individual was affected by various situations were identified and listed. Finally, members are asked to reflect and list their "part in it."

Members said that "I had to clean up my side of the street" and cease to justify their resentment or culpability. They endeavored to gain insight into their own actions, which made situations worse. Most members said that this exercise helped them to see how *they* were responsible for the things that had happened to them in the course of their lives. Alcoholics Anonymous stresses the extension of forgiveness to others in order to avoid the debilitating effects of resentment and hatred. As long as alcoholics nourish and hold on to their resentments, they are in danger of taking a drink. Most members said that this is an important aspect of the program and an integral part of the recovery process. Even though they know that they must, they said that they have trouble letting go of resentments because they are selfish.

Self-Centeredness

"Selfishness, self-centeredness! That is the root cause of all our problems" (AA 1976: 62). Everything revolves around self-centeredness. Fear is the most obvious fruit of selfishness. Usually it is the fear of losing something that we only think we have. The attendant worry and anxiety provide ample reason for the practicing alcoholic to drink. Amazingly, when first introduced to AA most members said that they did not think that they were especially self-centered. Some of them thought that it was patently ridiculous to suggest that they were interested only in themselves, since they could cite plenty of examples of their generosity and concern for others. They resisted the suggestion that they were self-centered. One member said that when he first read the Big Book he thought, "The idea that I was self-centered and that it was a problem was a real hoot." Another said that the suggestion that he was selfish was absolutely alien to his concept of himself. He may have appeared to be interested in himself sometimes, but he had specific justifications for all his actions. Almost all members concurred with the basic proposition that before they got sober, they didn't see themselves as particularly self-centered. They felt that they were just like everyone else around them. They were certainly on guard for things that might be of benefit to them and didn't want to let others run over them. After all, "You have to look out for yourself."

This behavior reflects the value of "looking out for number one" that is such an accepted attitude in modern America. Relations with employers, co-workers, business competitors, and associates are all conditioned to a certain extent by the prevailing attitude that "if you don't look out for yourself, nobody else will." This is a drastic contrast to the values in American society of mercy, sacrifice, and service to others. Contradictions such as this fuel the confusion of the practicing alcoholic. In the words of one woman, "When I walked into AA I didn't have nothing except the clothes on my back, and this guy came up to me and said, 'You know you're spoiled rotten, don't you.' I thought this guy must be crazy. But after being in the program for a while, I began to see that selfishness was my biggest problem."

Many members talked about how they wanted to be in control of everything and everyone around them. It is ironic, but altogether understandable, that individuals experiencing such loss of control over their own lives would be so concerned and compelled to maintain control over their own place in the environment. American society dearly values "self-control" and this plays an extremely important part in the denial syndrome.

Members continuously referred to the fact that they went so long before they sought any kind of assistance with their drinking problems because they wanted to show everyone, especially themselves, that they were capable of doing it on their own. They didn't need or want any help, and the suggestion that they could not control their own lives or behavior generated even lower self-esteem. Every time they lost control, they suffered the embarrassment of not practicing "the proper self-control." The more they lost control over their own behavior, the more they needed to control "all the actors in the play." In this way, other people were the cause of their frustration, and they increasingly medicated themselves with alcohol in order to escape the discomfort of not living up to their own expectations of themselves or the expectations of others. As one member put it, "I couldn't stand the fact that I was not getting the respect I felt I deserved." Many members often said that if everyone would just leave them alone, everything would be just fine.

Most AA members said that their selfishness just got worse as their dependence on alcohol increased. As they lost families, jobs, and their self-respect, they reacted by blaming their problems on others. They could not accept that they were out of control and totally self-centered. As the risk of death or madness became more apparent, they became even more obsessed with their *own* welfare. They needed someone else to blame. One member said, "When I first came into the program somebody told me to continue reading the Big Book after the 'How It Works' part on pages 62–63. I didn't really care for what it had to say because basically what it said was—I was the problem."

In the beginning many members found this concept to be very troublesome, but all said that as they worked the program, they began to see their part. Eventually, all members said that they had to realize that they were essentially selfish. They had to make an effort to accept responsibility for their own actions and learn to accept that "things aren't always going to go the way I want them to." Most members said that when they have an extreme attack of self-centeredness, they are in danger of taking a drink, and the best thing is to go to a meeting in order to try "to get out of myself." One member said that he is constantly finding out what a selfish person he is, and that it is an ongoing struggle to have enough humility to keep his sobriety. He said that "it seems like trying to stay sober, I'm practicing controlled self-centeredness and you know, it doesn't work much better than controlled drinking did." Just as members said that they had to give up the idea that they could drink normally, they also had to give up the idea that they should always put their own interests before the needs of others.

Levin addresses addiction as a disturbance of the self and details the narcissistic basis for alcoholism. "There are many reasons to consider alcoholism a disorder of the self. Alcoholism is, by definition, a form of self-destruction by self-poisoning, of suicide on the installment plan—a fact which strongly implies that alcoholism is a form of self-pathology. The alcoholic's notorious self-absorbtion is frequently highlighted both in the popular accounts and the scientific literature. In fact, one of AA's definitions of alcoholism is, 'self-will run riot'" (1987: 3). Paradoxically, the excessive self-centeredness of the alcoholic that readily develops under the influence of alcohol can lead to the destruction of the individual. The newcomer to AA is told he or she has to "give it up."

THE SOLUTION

Surrender

Hopeless, fearful, powerless, angry, resentful, and totally self-centered, most newcomers are ready to surrender. They were ready to "give up completely" when they entered the program. After denying that they were alcoholics, often for years, they were ready to admit that they were powerless over alcohol. After juggling family, friends, jobs, and drinking for long periods of time, they were ready to admit that they were unable to manage their own lives. After blaming everyone and everything imaginable for their problems rather than their own form of insanity, they became ready to accept the idea that they were responsible for their own situation. After repeatedly rejecting the notion that they needed help with their drinking or the conduct of their personal affairs, they were ready for someone or something to help them.

Members constantly talked about the absolute necessity of "giving it up completely." They had to surrender to the idea that they were alcoholic and begin to assimilate this new aspect of their identity into daily life. They had to surrender to alcohol. As more than one member said, "I fought alcohol all my life and alcohol won." They also had to surrender to the idea that they needed help to conquer all the adversity in their lives, not just the problem of alcohol dependence. They had to surrender, at least to the consideration, that only a power greater than themselves could restore them to sanity.

Many thought that they could not accept the concept of God on any basis. They were encouraged to look at the group dynamic as their higher power. The main object of such an exercise is that even if an individual has a problem with the concept of God, members said they still need some way to get outside themselves in order to recover. Many members said that they could see *something* working in the lives of other people in the program. These others, often with worse stories than their own, were miraculously recovering. In this way, they accepted the group dynamic as their higher power in the beginning.

One of the primary beliefs of most of those who recover from alcoholism in Alcoholics Anonymous is that only through a realization of the selfish nature of drinking life could they ever begin or continue to change. They had to replace the obsession with the self with a genuine concern for others. They had to depend on something outside of themselves, for they had not been able to manage life on their own. Members all agreed that it is critical to believe that there is some power outside the self that is more powerful than the individual. As one member said and others affirmed, "When I came into AA, I *had* to believe."

Members acknowledged that a total psychic change is necessary to recover from alcoholism. Such a total change and a radically different way of conceiving of the self were the products of surrendering old ideas and beliefs about the meaning and the challenge of life itself. Members said that in order to recover they had to believe Alcoholics Anonymous would work. They had to have "faith" that things would get better.

Faith

People who recover successfully in Alcoholics Anonymous say that in the beginning they had to give up the idea that they alone could take care of their problem. The typical member entered the program consumed by the negative perspective. When they do surrender they must do so with faith. They surrendered countless times to alcohol (Antze 1987). They tried to solve the problems they generated with a reliance "on the God of alcohol." It worked at first, but later it quit working. They had depended on alcohol. It had led them to a kind of insanity and to Alcoholics Anonymous. When they surrendered this time they had to surrender in faith. Paradoxically, they had to give up trying to control everything in order to regain control. They had to believe that only something outside of themselves could heal them.

In the program, a newcomer can look around and see that many people had similar problems and through working the program of AA that things improved. Most people had to believe that things would get better before they could accept that they had to completely change their way of thinking. They had to change the most basic propositions on which their belief system was founded and structured and which led them to make commitments to act. Many members that said at first they went to AA with no faith that it would work. They just did not believe that the program could be a solution for them. Many "went back out," only to return later. Many members said that when they finally came to AA and began "to get the program," they had to try and believe that it would be effective for it to begin to work. Finally, they said that they had to *accept* on faith that if they "did the things you people told me to do, it would get better."

Acceptance, Tolerance, and Patience

All members of AA with any significant length of sobriety will readily admit that they had to begin to practice acceptance in their daily lives in order to recover from alcoholism. When the Serenity Prayer—"God grant me the serenity to accept the things I cannot change, courage to change the things I can, and wisdom to know the difference"—is invoked it is an effective summary of one of the most important changes that they had to make in their system of belief.

Most people came to AA in fear, bewildered by the loss of control over their lives and their drinking. They harbored incredible resentments against all manner of people, places, institutions, situations, and things. They were unable to accept their behavior, but they were equally unable to end the denial that allowed them to practice their alcoholism. They believed that they simply did not have to accept anything that provoked them. They wanted to be "the director of the play." They worried about things over which they had no control. They could not accept their alcoholism, their financial situation, their marriage or their divorce, their poverty or their affluence, and they could not accept themselves as a part of any community. They felt isolated and alone.

Acceptance is a key concept, since when one practices acceptance there is no urge to control everything, or get upset when things don't go a certain way and drink over it. It is also critically important to many who are agnostic, atheist, or otherwise "have problems with" the "God, as we understand" concept. During a meeting in which the topic of doing God's will was discussed, one woman stated that she had never been able to believe in God or deal with the concept. She found it difficult to believe in God, at least all the conceptions of God that she had heard. But she said that early in the program, she had "latched onto the concept of acceptance." She discovered that as she became more accepting and more tolerant of others, she was less likely to become upset. She said that this attitude made it easier for her to abstain from using alcohol and also improved the quality of her daily life. Acceptance had become her God.

It is apparent that one of the functions of the meetings, especially with the rule against "cross talk," is providing the chance to exercise tolerance and patience. Individuals must sit and suffer through all manner of opinions with which they may not agree. Allowing everyone to have their say and learning to really listen, members practice patience, acceptance, and tolerance. Through this practice they gain understanding and insight into others and the self. Just sitting through the meeting and listening, whether one wants to or not, can be severely distressing to the newcomer or the regular member. Sometimes extreme patience is required. Once members began to practice acceptance, their problems did not disappear, but they were able to more fully and productively deal with situations in daily life. Some felt that they should have some means to measure "just how much of this shit I'm going to take." This was a mistake that many newcomers made. Members said that they had to realize that they were dependent on many things, that they were *not God*, that they were human and sometimes needed help, that they were alcoholic, that they needed to work these steps, that they needed to change their whole way of thinking, and that they needed to go to meetings from time to time to remind themselves where they came from. And this is just a partial list of the things they needed to accept.

This is a lot to choke down if you are new to the program of Alcoholics Anonymous or even if you have been in AA for years. People consistently expressed the belief that the development of true acceptance cannot come all at once, but it is a continuing process. Futhermore, it is constantly pointed out in meetings that the only way to get started on such a behavioral process and to continue to examine the interior life is to become more honest, open, and willing "to do the things I need to do" in order to change.

Honesty, Openness, and Willingness

Alcoholics Anonymous can only be effective if the individual is committed to working the program in the spirit of honesty, openness, and willingness. Many people may have reservations about God or about others providing direction for their attitudes and behavior. Newcomers and regulars alike are encouraged to be open about new ideas, honest about their feelings, and willing to try a different approach. Many members said that when they came to AA they thought that they were some of the most honest and open people on the face of the earth. Whatever their problems, they did not feel that they were closed-minded or inherently dishonest. But, many of these same people said that as they began to attend meetings, they were able to re-examine their attitudes, values, and beliefs from a different perspective due to the altered state of consciousness that had been induced by not drinking. Once they quit using alcohol, they began to view themselves in a different way. They began to see themselves as an integral part of the world around them rather than as an autonomous entity.

Members often contrasted the "cash register" honesty that they had practiced in the past with the interior honesty that is fostered in the program of Alcoholics Anonymous. As they opened themselves to this new view, they began to see past behaviors and beliefs in a new context. They also asserted that this process of searching for the truth led them to open themselves further to the wisdom of others. On this basis, most of them concluded that they needed to continue to open themselves to new ideas in order to discover the truth about themselves. They said that as a result of this process, they became more honest with themselves. As one member said, "I was real good at fooling people when I was drinking and I knew it, but when I got sober I realized that the one I had been fooling the worst was myself." Members said that in order to engage in the process of change, they had to become willing.

Willingness is identified by members as the necessary prerequisite to carrying out most of the suggested actions of the AA program. They had to become willing to try and they had to become willing in order to change. As many members said throughout the course of this study, "I had to become willing to become willing." So many of the concepts, attitudes, beliefs, values, and actions that are suggested as a program of recovery in Alcoholics Anonymous appear to be impossible to the newcomer and remain extremely problematic to the developing member. In order to accept these suggestions on a practical level, individuals are counselled to "just become willing" to try the rest of the program. Willingness led them to new openness, which in turn led to more complete honesty. Through the honest assessment of their values, beliefs, and behaviors they were able to accept the 12-step program on a practical level, which became an effective behavior modification program.

In many ways, the first five steps of the AA program specifically address the problems of hopelessness, powerlessness, fear, anger, and resentment. By being willing to become more open and honest, the AA member began to surrender, and these difficulties began to dissipate as acceptance, tolerance, and patience led to an increase in faith. They began to have more faith that the program could work for them, and they began to really believe that they had been living in error. They had been living with the paradox of an extremely exaggerated sense of self while they suffered from low self-esteem. As members fondly and repeatedly stated, "An alcoholic is an egomaniac with an inferiority complex." They had been filled with alcoholic pride and had no humility.

Humility

Members of Alcoholics Anonymous recognize that the 12-step program changes the way people see themselves in relation to others. As newcomers began to change and became more aware of others, they began to feel as if they were an integral part of the world, rather than the center of life on this planet. Members said that they

began to realize that their ego, pride, jealousy, envy, greed, and a host of other
destructive feelings had interfered with the sense of self and destroyed their peace
of mind. They began to see themselves in interaction with a world that was
substantially different than the world that they had constructed with their old ideas.
They no longer assumed that they were, in fact, the center of the known universe.
Members said that they began to see things "more as they really are, instead of the
way I want them to be."

Many members were totally humiliated by the time they made a successful effort
to get sober. As they became less self-centered, they made progress in accepting
things as they are and surrendered a little further to a power greater than themselves.
They acknowledged with openness and honsety their dependence on matters that
were outside the realm of personal power. They humbled themselves to accept their
limitations as human beings and the fact that they are not God. Once they began to
practice some measure of humility and dedication to the truth, they were able to
clearly examine the personal shortcomings that they had discovered as a result of
a "searching and fearless moral inventory" (step 4), in which they had "admitted to
God, to ourselves, and to another human being the exact nature of our wrongs" (step
5). They could see more clearly how their attitudes, beliefs, behaviors, past actions,
and the daily interactions they experienced had been determined and would
continue to be determined to a great extent by the character defects that they had
discovered through these steps.

Character Defects

Character defects are frequently introduced as a topic at discussion meetings and
refer specifically to steps six ("We were entirely ready to have God remove all these
defects of character") and seven ("Humbly asked Him to remove our shortcomings"). Members stressed that they have to get rid of these "defects" in order
to maintain sobriety as a way of life. The first and most important defect that they
addressed is the compulsion to drink. They said that their alcoholic thinking always
led them to believe that the answer to some frustration, anxiety, or situation in life
could best be found by "taking a drink." Yet, most considered this defect to be the
result of more basic defects that contributed to the compulsion. By the time the AA
member has reached these steps, members said that the compulsion to take a drink
will have largely disappeared. They claim that it has been removed by a higher
power. As one member said, "God removed the compulsion to drink. There are still
a lot of times when my thinking gets messed up, and I think about taking a drink,
but that's all it is, a thought, not a compulsion. Since that compulsion has been
removed I can have a second thought, and my second thought is always that I don't
have to drink over it."

Members suggested that if God removed this defect, it should certainly be able
to remove the basic and lasting defects that contributed to alcohol dependence. If
not directly addressed, these defects can prevent the individual from realizing a
lasting and quality sobriety. Members said that defects of character originated in the
seven deadly sins. Pride, greed, anger, lust, gluttony, envy, and sloth are excessive

responses to the natural needs and desires of human beings. They form the foundation for defects that interfere with our usefulness to ourselves and others and contribute to the development of alcoholism. If these tendencies are not removed, the individual in recovery is bound to fail to remain sober.

Products of these basic flaws, such as fear, worry, resentment, and self-centeredness feed alcoholic thinking. Members stressed that these defects of character have to be removed. They also stressed that the individual can no more remove them by an act of willpower, than they could remove the compulsion to drink. They have to ask God in order to be relieved of them, and if they cannot, they are in constant danger of losing sobriety. As with most other aspects of the program, the experienced member always referred to the continuous process of removing one's character defects. They cautioned the newcomer that all these defects will not be removed simply by asking. Members must be constantly aware when these defects surface and should engage in meditation and prayer to be relieved of them once more. Here again, gradual progress is the key, and members claim that progress can only be realized if the 12-step program of Alcoholics Anonymous is approached "one day at a time."

One Day at a Time

Staying sober "one day at a time" was often cited by members as the only road to recovery. Most said that guilt and shame regarding past behavior kept them practicing their alcoholism. Many claimed that their failure to "control" their drinking and their lives led them to rely more desperately on alcohol. Many also claimed that fear, worry, and anxiety about the future also contributed significantly to their dependence on alcohol. In order to deal with this anxiety about the past or the future, they depended on alcohol more extensively.

Members frequently said that they have to live in the present and simply "do what's put in front of me." They cannot afford to worry excessively about the wrongs they have committed in the past. They can only become "willing to make amends to all those we have harmed" (step 8) and try "to make direct amends wherever possible, except when to do so would injure them or others" (step 9). Newcomers are cautioned by more experienced members that they should not expect to be able to undo all the damage right away. They have to make amends willingly and to the best of their ability. In a true spirit of contrition, they "have to let go and let God" handle the specifics. As far as the future is concerned, they cannot afford to engage in useless anxiety over what might happen to them tomorrow, but they can take care of today. In addition to learning how this concept applies to the steps of the program, they must also concentrate on "not taking a drink today." In the realm of the present day, it is impossible to not take a drink tomorrow.

Many members said that one of the problems they initially had with the AA program, even though they realized they needed to do something about their drinking, was that they simply "couldn't imagine life without alcohol." They had become so dependent that they did not see how it was possible. Since the AA program is intended to initiate and sustain a lifetime of abstinence, many thought that they could not "hope to go the rest of life without a drink." In the beginning, many newcomers felt that this was an impossible task, became depressed, and continued to drink—giving the program an opportunity to succeed.

Everyone at the club with any significant time in sobriety readily admitted that it was only the concept of "one day at a time" that allowed real hope for a future as an abstinent individual. Most people who came to AA were seriously dependent on alcohol to manage most of the stresses, feelings, and emotions they experienced daily. The habit of taking a drink to medicate these emotions was so strong that they were constantly assaulted by the compulsion to drink. Even those who said that the compulsion to take a drink was relieved in the beginning were still subject to the thought. And the thought of going the rest of one's life without a drink can be defeating. Yet with the goal of "a daily reprieve" as a measurement of success, success is attainable today. People felt that they had a chance to be successful in the program on a daily basis. Eventually these days turned into weeks, months, years, and decades of sobriety. By keeping one's focus on today, the individual is able to postpone the decision to drink and hope that the compulsion will leave. Members said that it is only by working the program one day at a time can the alcoholic "keep it simple" enough to have a chance to succeed.

Keep It Simple

The admonition to "keep it simple" specifically referred most often to the program of AA, but also to life itself. As it says in "How It Works" in the Big Book, "Those who do not recover are people who cannot or will not completely give themselves to this simple program" (AA 1976: 58). It is regarded as somewhat of a heresy to suggest that the AA program is anything but simple. Members cautioned newcomers that they can make all the principles of AA extraordinarily complex if they aren't careful. They said that they tended to have problems when they didn't keep it simple enough, that simplicity is the main reason for the program's great success, and that efforts to complicate the process will lead to failure. Many said that they want to complicate things, rationalize things, or worry about things, and this is an impediment to the successful transformation to a sober life-style. They claimed that the program is a very straightforward guide for how to achieve and maintain sobriety and that any efforts to make it more complex will probably meet with failure.

Members exhorted newcomers and established members alike to work the program in a simple manner. By applying AA to daily life, they said that it will also become easier for them to live in a less complicated manner. Members repeatedly said, "It's in the book," gave the page number, and quoted the relevant passage anytime someone expressed confusion about a certain aspect of behavior or belief. Yet, while suggesting that simplicity can aid greatly in sobriety, almost all admitted that it is their nature and their habit to want more extensive and satisfying explanations for their experiences in life. In a way, it was also keeping it very simple that led them to dependence on alcohol. They simply reached for the bottle anytime they were confused, agitated, or in a mood to celebrate.

The AA program is one of adamant simplicity, but paradoxically, for many members the effort to keep it simple leads to a much more intellectually satisfying explanation of their place in the world. As human beings we are biologically, emotionally, and mentally capable of handling extraordinary amounts of information, which is essential to our continued existence as individuals, in groups, and as a species. Children begin to learn language by generalizing and simplifying. Through such generalizing behavior they begin to structure their experience into categories. The development of such categorical structures is not only necessary for a child to learn language, but it is also necessary for a person to develop a belief system that determines the types of behaviors that are appropriate in various situations. These guidelines act as rules that help us understand how to behave and are part of enculturation into the group. In the same way, the AA member is assisted in simplifying and generalizing in new ways about the appropriateness of their beliefs and behavior. They are led to reorganize information within and between categories.

Not only is this ability to generalize important to language learning, enculturation, and participation in a cultural group; it is also necessary to adaptation and acculturation. This ability is the gift of human existence. The alcoholic's task in AA is to be able to simplify and generalize about his or her experience with alcohol in order to discover new insight into the effect of drinking on his or her beliefs and behavior. Although AA members must keep it simple, they have to accept the complex nature of existence on this planet without wanting or needing to control this complexity. New generalizations allow members to reorganize category structure. This must lead to the transformation of belief or they will probably "slip" in their efforts to not drink and suffer relapse.

Slips

Relapses are commonly referred to as "slips" by most AA members. Most people agreed that this word is indicative of the "cunning, baffling and powerful" nature of alcohol dependence. Stories abound in which someone who is trying to abstain suddenly orders a drink. Many times, this type of falling back into drinking was described in such a way as to suggest that some external power or force led them to pick up a drink. However, many members also talk of having slips because they simply could not handle the compulsion to drink. So they made a conscious decision to drink.

Members' stories in the meetings relate the varied nature of the slip and the circumstances that surrounded it. In most cases, the individual was having difficulty with other aspects of life and made the decision to take a drink in an attempt to handle the problem the old way. In other cases, a favorable occurrence in life led to taking a drink in celebration. Whether due to a good or bad happening, the overwhelming majority of people in the program have experienced one or more slips. Generally, they expressed the belief that to a certain extent the episode was out of their control. However, there is a very vocal minority of members who, when asked to express their feelings on slips, will tell the group that they have never experienced a slip, but have made conscious, well-thought decisions to drink while in the midst of working the AA program. These people insist that it was simply a matter of finding an excuse or not needing an excuse to take a drink. They were simply reverting to the alcoholic thinking that got them to AA to start with. Most said that their screwed up thinking enabled them to pick up that first drink. Others suggested that this kind of thinking is just another way to take "control" of their drinking.

Many members describe relapses as an inability by the alcoholic to fully accept the new identity of an alcoholic and truly believe they can never take another drink. The most common relapse is one that occurs within the first year or two of abstinence. This situation is best characterized by the developmental model of alcoholism reported by Brown (1985). In her model, alcoholics in AA have to go through various stages of development to achieve an abstinent lifestyle. She reports that in early sobriety, frequent relapses are the rule and suggests that it is part of the development of an alcoholic identity. Most members experienced slips during this early period of time in the program. After they had made the mental transition and accepted the tenet of AA that claims that they will never be able to drink successfully, these episodic relapses tended to diminish significantly and then disappear completely. While they do occur, they have a definite function within the alcoholic community of the AA group.

Newcomers are repeatedly told that slips can be expected, especially, "if you're not really working the steps." This is particularly true if "you haven't really taken step one, 100 percent." Step one is the "only step we have to take all the way," to succeed in maintaining sobriety. Many newcomers have great success at the beginning because they are so close to the painful experiences that led them through the doors of AA. They began to "work the program," go to meetings, and not drink. As the altered state of consciousness—called sobriety—began to take effect, they felt that the compulsion to drink had been removed. Often these individuals were more content than they had been in years. They had new hope for their lives and they expressed it at meetings. They experienced a kind of sober intoxication.

Unfortunately, many established members who had experienced similar feelings and then had subsequent slips themselves began to caution the newcomer that they were on a "pink cloud" and had better be wary and re-dedicate themselves to really "working the program." This can condition the newcomer to expect a renewed period of depression as inevitable and a relapse as an almost invariable result. Since newcomers have heard these other successful members telling them to expect this consequence, they may accept the compulsion to drink as a part of the recovery process. In this way, the negative talk about pink clouds can be very detrimental to members trying to maintain abstinence. The newcomer can relapse more readily because it is *expected*. These admonitions to quit feeling so happy can be a self-fulfilling prophesy.

Some researchers have suggested that those who do relapse and return to problem drinking are fulfilling a prophesy in much the same way, because of the things they have heard in the meetings that indicate that they will have problems again if they return to drinking (Heather and Robertson 1988). However, almost all the people in this study claimed that when they did return to drinking, they were at first successful because they were aware of the problem. They were able to drink for a while without incident and this encouraged them to further reject the AA dogma. Eventually, they again lost control and began to experience the same set of problem behaviors that led them to AA. Many times people simply cannot believe that they need to stay sober. They want to have fun and drink with others. They want to be a part of the crowd again. They need to discover on their own, empirically, as they have before that they cannot control their intake of alcohol or their behavior when intoxicated. It is often said in meetings that "AA ruined my drinking." This is the experience of many who "go back out" after a period of abstinence in the program of AA. They simply don't have as much fun as they used to because they are constantly on guard to control their drinking and their behavior.They cannot achieve the release and relaxation that alcohol afforded them in the past. As a result, they return to the program with a new acceptance of themselves as "somebody who just can't drink."

There are also relapses of those who had significant periods of sobriety. These are some of the most tragic stories. After a period of years these people return to drinking. One member was fond of recalling that he had four years of sobriety in Alcoholics Anonymous when one day he went to the store for a six-pack, "and it took me 16 years to get back." Almost all the regular members who had experienced relapses said that they would not have had a relapse if they had been working the program the way it was supposed to be worked. Almost any discussion of slips in an AA meeting will focus on the steps. Many members maintained that it is impossible to have a slip if one is "working a step that day." If the member is not working actively on the steps, then he or she is in danger of a relapse. In order to maintain sobriety, "you have to work the steps."

MAINTENANCE

Working the Steps

The steps are the basic action suggested as a program of recovery. Established members repeatedly recommended "working the program" to the newcomer, to the person developing early sobriety, and to other established members. Members said that a person can want to get sober desperately and stay that way, but if he or she is not working the steps to the best of his or her ability, then that person is in danger of "going back out."

The more hardcore AA members, who tend to be more dogmatic, said that "you have to work the steps and you have to work them in order." Almost all members agreed that the steps were written in the order they appear because that is generally the way they need to be approached. However, some claimed to work whatever step they could regardless of the order. In the early development of Alcoholics Anonymous (AA 1976: 292) there were only six steps: (1) complete deflation, (2) dependence and guidance from a higher power, (3) moral inventory, (4) confession,

(5) restitution, and (6) continued work with other alcoholics. The steps were later elaborated and refined after early AA members had the benefit of some practical experience. Early members discovered that one could not simply go through the steps and be cured, but that the entire process had to be ongoing and progressive.

Although it is always recommended that the individual make every effort to work the steps as completely as possible, there is a great deal of variability in the way that one may work the steps. This is one of the strengths of the 12-step program. It is flexible enough to accommodate a large and diverse population. Many members said that they did not really complete the steps concerning inventory, confession, and restitution, but they did them to the best of their ability and rely on a combination of the steps concerning surrender, insight, and maintenance to stay sober.

Contrary to the dogmatic and inflexible approach to the steps exhibited by some, most people approached the steps in a spirit of individual variation, which is required for the program to be effective for a large number of people. As many members said, "Alcoholics Anonymous is like a cafeteria. You take what you like and leave the rest on the shelf," and maybe a hunger will develop for it later. An inflexible attitude may not be helpful, or it may even be dangerous, for some newcomers who cannot accept that everyone has to work the program in a particular way. This inflexible attitude is directly contrary to the principles of the program, but since AA is full of human beings who make errors from time to time, it happens. There are untrained individuals who offer advice to the newcomer and insist that he or she must follow directions. Unfortunately newcomers may be alienated by such individuals.

There are many more sober members of AA who recognize the real flexibility of the program concerning amends, inventories, and confessions. They realize that everyone is different. There are also a few members, some of whom sponsor people, who feel that a person may begin to work the program wherever possible. One thing is certain; all sober members of AA feel that one must make the effort to take the action revealed in the steps. As one member is fond of saying, "You have to act your way into better thinking. You can't think your way into better acting."

Members also frequently mentioned that they felt extremely lucky to have been an alcoholic and exposed to the steps of the program. They claim that it is a good guide for daily living, one that seeks to enhance understanding, usefulness, self-esteem, and happiness. They said that if they hadn't been alcoholics, they would have never known. They indicated that the 12-step program can be applied to anyone's daily life. This flexibility is obviously the reason that other groups have successfully adapted the 12 steps to other behavioral disorders. Everyone cannot completely carry out the action of the steps, but the idea is that if people work the steps to the best of their ability, they will see changes in what they believe and how they react. Their attitudes will change and they will begin to "intuitively know how to handle situations that used to baffle" them (AA 1976: 84). This is the promise of the AA fellowship.

Fellowship of the Program

AA members typically replaced drinking with the fellowship of Alcoholics Anonymous. Meetings on this topic generally center on all the activities in which they engage relative to AA. Some cautioned that early in their sobriety they tried to get along on the fellowship alone. "Just suit up and show up" is a frequent topic. They maintained that unless one is working the steps, the fellowship will do nothing. Obviously, many newcomers are confused about all these new concepts. Initially, they are able to use the meetings for fellowship, so that they can be away from bars and drunks. At AA they can hang around with someone sober. There are many members who make their phone numbers available for anyone to call when they have a problem. The fellowship is critical and apparently more critical in the early development of sobriety. Newcomers go to many more meetings than old timers. Newer members are more involved in club sponsored activities and develop more friendships with other members.

The biggest strength of Alcoholics Anonymous is having a number of abstinent individuals with a history of drinking problems with which to discuss the relative advantages of sobriety and a practical way it can be achieved and maintained. The fellowship provides a new social network within which to live and interact. It becomes unnecessary to proceed to a drinking environment in order to maintain some sense of social relations. For years, alcoholics became progressively more dependent on alcohol and the environment in which alcohol was consumed. Often, the only friends they had left were those who consumed even more alcohol and had more problems than they did. The fellowship provides social stimulus and a way to forge new relationships that are not dependent on alcohol related activities.

The fellowship is a source of ideas and a tremendous catalyst for a change of attitude, action, awareness, and understanding. Most important, it provides a speech community with a different set of principles embedded in its specialized language than the larger community. It provides the cultural milieu by which a different set of meanings is acquired for previous behaviors. Drinking behavior is viewed very differently from the confines of AA culture. Its members come to believe that alcohol has caused them to suffer. Their inability to stop drinking was replaced with a practical method to change their beliefs and their behavior. This change in the perception of the self, others, and the world is the message they wish to convey to other alcoholics.

Carrying the Message

Many AA members exhibit unmitigated, missionary zeal about carrying the message of Alcoholics Anonymous. Many became obsessed with spreading this message. One member said that during the first three years of sobriety, "I went around hitting people over the head with the Big Book and dragging people that I thought needed it, into meetings of AA." During this time, he tried to carry the message to a lot of people who were not alcoholics and "didn't need it." He learned that he didn't need to push the program on anyone, so he "quit promoting it" which is in accord with the traditions of AA. Over the years he became comfortable with the fact that "God would put in front of" him "the opportunity to help other alcoholics" but that he could only share his experience with them. He stressed that he could not control what other people heard and he alone could not heal them anymore than they could heal themselves.

When people listen to an alcoholic tell about his or her experience, they do not all hear the same thing. The things to which they assign significance vary considerably. Many people in the program talk about coming to meetings and hearing the same thing repeatedly before the significance of the utterance ever became apparent to them. Many of them said that it was amazing that they ever understood anything and that every time they attended a meeting they were carrying the message that "miracles" happen in Alcoholics Anonymous.

Miracles

Most members said, "just the fact that I'm here rather than at a bar, drunk somewhere is a miracle." They almost invariably felt that their lives were such as mess that it truly was a "miracle" that they were sober. Many talked of the incredible fact that they are still alive and able to do anything, since many of their drinking escapades were life threatening. The "promises" of the Big Book are often cited as miracles:

We are going to know a new freedom and a new happiness. We will not regret the past nor wish to shut the door on it. We will comprehend the word serenity and we will know peace. No matter how far down the scale we have gone, we will see how our experience can benefit others. That feeling of uselessness and self-pity will disappear. We will lose interest in selfish things and gain interest in our fellows. Self-seeking will slip away. Our whole attitude and outlook on life will change. Fear of people and of economic insecurity will leave us. We will intuitively know how to handle situations which used to baffle us. We will suddenly realize that God is doing for us what we could not do for ourselves. (AA 1976: 83-84)

This passage is often read or cited by members as indicative of the way that things can be if the alcoholic can remain sober and work the steps of the program.

Many dogmatic AA members insist that one must achieve at least partial completion of the ninth step in the program and finish making the amends they need to make in order for these promises to begin to come true, but many members claim that miracles began to occur in their lives immediately upon making a sincere effort to work the steps. Some said that they began to experience miracles in their lives as soon as they became abstinent. Generally, members of AA came to have serious personal, social, financial, physical, and mental problems in life due to increasing dependence on alcohol. It is no wonder that many of these individuals say that they began to experience miraculous things once they quit drinking. For most, just the fact that they have been able to function in daily life without medicating themselves to drunkenness is the biggest miracle. After years of reaching for a drink in order to deal with some aspect of life, they found that they do not have to resist alcohol, since the temptation to drink is substantially removed. This miracle of successful abstinence and the dramatic improvements they perceived in their lives led most members to be extremely thankful. They are grateful to be alive, sober, and of some use to the other people in their lives.

Gratitude

It is extremely difficult to find any AA members who do not feel that life is better sober, than drunk. No matter what difficulties they may be experiencing in daily existence, these pale compared to the problems that they encountered as practicing alcoholics. Given the extent of problems associated with the use of alcohol, it is easy to see how even people who may be unemployed or having family problems can focus on being thankful that they are not drinking.

Most discussions of gratitude center on how people became dissatisfied, both when they were drinking and when they were sober. They became upset because of all the old ideas still in their heads. They forgot what a terrible time they had when they were drinking. By focusing on what it was like before, they can generate the necessary gratitude to maintain their sobriety. They are often grateful that "taking a drink is not a solution" for any problem. They remember when they used to "drink over everything" and when it quit working. As one member said, "Some days things are so bad that all I can do is just be grateful I'm not drinking." Here are some of the things for which various members said they were grateful during one meeting:

. . . for sobriety one day at a time
. . . have been kept sober by a power greater than myself
. . . now I have hope, and that I didn't have to lose everything
. . . now I'm alive and sober and grateful for that, because before I wasn't grateful for nothing and now I have the fellowship
. . . who knows what kind of bad things would have happened to me in the last year if I had been drinking
. . . the people who have been sober a long time are just grateful to be sober today
. . . now that I've been sober for two years, I can do things like brush my teeth and comb my hair
. . . I went to a lot of groups, but here is where I felt comfortable and was able to get sober
. . . when I came in I was depressed and all my relationships had been affected by drinking, I used to think it was everyone else, but in sobriety I can see that it was me, and now all my relationships are getting better and I've even made some friends
. . . I don't have a chip on my shoulder any more
. . . these simple ideas have helped me deal with some terrible experiences in sobriety, but I know it would be worse if I was drunk
. . . and I'm just grateful to be here
. . . for my belief in God.

Alcoholic thinking gives way to a different way of believing and living through the *process of healing* in AA. This process of healing is paradoxical in many respects. By giving up the compulsion to be in control of everything, AA members realize more actual control over their lives. By accepting dependence on a power greater than themselves and on others around them, they achieve the functional independence that had eluded them earlier. By caring for the welfare of others, they are more able to care for themselves. By becoming grateful for what little they have, they obtain much more for which to give thanks. By becoming willing to consider how little they really understand about God, they come to believe. Through this process they are changed and healed.

7

Language, Culture, and Belief

OUTCOME OF THE HEALING PROCESS IN ALCOHOLICS ANONYMOUS

Alcohol use is the most prevalent, expensive, socially and personally disruptive drug problem in the United States. Over the past 60 years, Alcoholics Anonymous has been effective in helping hundreds of thousands of people to recover from this hopeless state of mind and body. Despite the success of AA, the organization probably only reaches approximately 5 percent of the total population of alcohol dependent individuals in this country. Other treatment alternatives only reach a comparably small proportion of alcoholics. The number of alcoholics in the United States continues to grow, and the estimated number of alcohol abusers remains stable, even though every year many individuals recover or die (NIAAA 1990). The problem is becoming more severe in spite of our efforts to reach an effective solution.

Alcoholics Anonymous is effective as a *community of healers*. Although many researchers have questioned the efficacy of AA as a therapeutic alternative to treat alcoholism, it is clear from this ethnography that many individuals have experienced a significant measure of healing through the 12-step program and the fellowship of Alcoholics Anonymous. Through this study we have seen that members of AA are bound together by their common experience with alcoholism and through the shared system of beliefs developed as a solution to the problem. It is a cultural group that proposes a spiritual program of living to overcome the difficulties of daily life as well as dependence on alcohol. It is not a religious organization, although some members may very well use the program as the basis for a ritualized personal theology and morality. The community recognizes the sociocultural and individual factors that lead to the development of alcohol abuse and dependence. It recognizes the role of attitudes, values, and beliefs that are highly esteemed in contemporary American culture that encourage the use of alcohol and foster dependence. And it realizes that these beliefs contribute to the actions of individuals, actions that seem to be characteristic of behavioral problems associated with alcoholism. The community of Alcoholics Anonymous suggests that transformation of belief is the only effective long-term solution to alcoholism. The changing world view among recovering alcoholics in AA is essential to the healing process.

Goodenough (1990) characterizes beliefs as a set of propositions that form the basis for a commitment to action. In his discussion on the evolution of the human capacity for beliefs, he contends that until human beings were capable of language, through which they could develop such sets of propositions, they could not have had the capacity for beliefs. In much the same way, alcoholics in the program of AA must develop a new set of propositions on which to base beliefs that can lead to a change in behavior. This is accomplished mostly through verbal repetition at AA meetings. Repeatedly, they are offered new meanings for old terms and concepts. This redundancy is obvious in reading this report and has become in itself a level of explanation as well as description. Gradually, but dramatically, information is reordered within the category structures of the individual. From such reorganization, new sets of propositions emerge, which form a new and different basis for a commitment to not only behavioral action, but most importantly to symbolic action as well.

As AA members learn to manipulate this new referential system, they acquire a radically different foundation for the symbolic representation of reality. Their whole way of thinking and believing is transformed. They utilize this new perception in order to better understand themselves and to interpret the world. Initially, they desire to change in order to achieve abstinence from alcohol, but later they discover that the principles of this new system of belief lead to a new conception of life. They teach that only through practicing these principles in all of their affairs can they hope to maintain sobriety. In this way Alcoholics Anonymous can be an effective method of healing and is similar to other traditional systems of folk medicine. As Victor Turner states, "The healing rite in 'folk' or 'tribal' medicine is seen to be more than the typing and labelling of diseases and symptoms and the restoration of health. It is rather the mobilization of efficacy through symbolic action for restoring internal integrity to the patient and order to his community" (Turner 1975: 159). This is an accurate description of the AA approach to healing alcoholics. Members are engaged in the restoration of their own physical and mental health, but they believe that recovery can only be achieved through a conceptual (spiritual) awakening that restores their own internal integrity and enables them to become useful to other people in their families and communities.

Behavior modification applied to drinking is only one aspect of healing in AA. The 12-step program requires the individual to change behavior in many areas of daily life, but the action of the program as a process of change is substantially symbolic. Much of the suggested action in the steps is symbolic action. Prayer, meditation, surrender, moral inventory, confession, making amends, and helping others all involve behavioral modifications that may constitute action, but they also require the integration of action that is symbolic. Members may have to take time to kneel and pray, sit comfortably to meditate, and not take a drink to surrender in the battle with alcohol, but all these exercises have greater efficacy as specific actions that symbolize the willingness to depend on a power greater than themselves rather than their own personal power. Making a moral inventory and confession involve direct actions, but they are more important as they symbolize acceptance of the past as it really was rather than the illusion they wanted it to be. Making amends or extending restitution may involve paying back money or apologizing in an attempt to restore someone's peace of mind, but they are most important as a symbol of genuine contrition and a reminder of past behavior that may have harmed others. Helping others may involve actually going to hospitals or homes and devoting time, money, and energy to the task, but these efforts are symbolic of the gratitude they have for the "gift of sobriety."

The steps are symbolic of the personal transformation that the individual must experience. Most members readily admit that no one ever really completes the steps and recognize the program as an ongoing process in which they are becoming transformed. As members of Alcoholics Anonymous, they identify with each other as human beings who are changing, developing, and getting better. Much of the emphasis on behavioral modification therapy as a solution to alcohol dependence misses this point.

Levinson correctly emphasizes the importance of recognizing cultural factors in the treatment of alcoholism, but he mistakenly constructs an argument that behavior modification is most effective and desired because it is less likely to disturb an individual's cultural identity. He states, "Behavior modification treatment . . . compared to other treatment approaches such as Alcoholics Anonymous . . . probably do less damage to cultural identities of the individuals receiving treatment. Alcoholics Anonymous, in particular, implicitly requires members to give up their cultural identity and adopt the identity of AA member or recovered alcoholic (1983: 256).

While this new cultural identity may pose problems in extending the AA program to some ethnic groups within American society or different traditional cultures around the world, it is not representative of subjects in this study. People in Alcoholics Anonymous are no more "implicitly required" to give up their primary cultural identity than are sports fans. For example, just because someone is an avid football, baseball, basketball, or hockey fan does not mean he or she must give up being an American, Hispanic American, African American, Asian American, or Native American. Many individuals in the complex society of the United States are bicultural and some may even be tricultural. Membership in one group does not preclude simultaneous membership in the larger society or membership in additional cultural groups. Members view their inclusion in the fellowship of AA as complimentary to their membership in American culture or other important ethnic or otherwise distinctively cultural groups. Levinson continues, "Second, because behavior modification treatments focus on drinking behaviors and behaviors associated with drinking, other behaviors, which are often culturally patterned such as relationships among family members, are left relatively undisturbed" (1983: 256). From what I have learned during the course of recovery and this study, these are *precisely the relationships* that have *already* been *severely disturbed due to the culturally patterned development and practice of alcoholism.*

Such an approach does not address the underlying problem played by cultural assumptions regarding the attitudes, values, and beliefs upon which the alcoholic bases behavior. Members of AA said that it was critical to extensively modify their personal and cultural identities in order to change their perception of reality. Nor does it take into account that members of AA think that it is necessary to qualitatively change their relationships with virtually everyone and everything in order to recover. For many alcoholics in AA, nothing could be worse than leaving their relationships "intact," as they were when they were drinking. Finally, behavior modification involves very little symbolic action, which is required to effectively transform the belief system and world view that supported drinking and associated behaviors.

Medical therapies treat the body and behavior modification treats the mind, but members of Alcoholics Anonymous recognize alcoholism as an affliction of the mind, body, and spirit. They see it holistically as a total illness. Members of AA contend that unless the underlying perception of reality is changed through the symbolic action of the steps, they cannot hope for a lasting and quality sobriety. AA members said that even if they manage to not drink, unfortunately, they will probably experience life as a "dry drunk." This term is used by members to characterize abstinence in the context of hanging on to the same "old ideas," the same self-centered behavior without the alcohol, and even though less acute, the similar personal problems of confusion, suffering, discontent, and even despair.

Alcoholics Anonymous helps people with alcohol dependence by offering assistance in a spirit of tolerance, patience, and acceptance. It encourages individuals to open themselves to a new process of living, thinking, feeling, and believing. Among other things, it fosters love, generosity, duty, responsibility, and freedom. And it can work.

AN ANTHROPOLOGICAL THEORY OF ALCOHOLISM AND RECOVERY

Ruth Bunzel (1940) first noted the importance of the cultural contexts in which alcohol was used and the apparent differences in the meanings of drinking and drunkenness. Shortly thereafter, Donald Horton (1943) pioneered broad-based, crosscultural comparisons in order to determine why people drink and especially, to predict why people might drink to a state of drunkenness. Since then, anthropologists have developed many hypothetical constructs to explain variation in drinking and drunkenness in different cultures. Such investigations have made very important contributions to the study of the worldwide production, use, and abuse of alcoholic beverages.

Past anthropological work can provide an important basis for comparison and analysis of the data generated by this study of alcoholics who have recovered from alcohol dependence in the 12-step program of Alcoholics Anonymous. Through careful consideration of what we have learned in anthropology over the past 50 years about the relationship of human beings and cultures to alcoholic beverages, we may be able to apply the data that is now accessible from alcoholics in AA to an anthropological theory of the development and practice of alcoholism and recovery. We must also take into account the psychological, medical, and sociological work that has contributed to our knowledge of alcohol dependence as it is currently understood. Using these data and the important theoretical constructs of culture, adaptation, and evolution as they apply to human behavior, it may be possible to develop a theory of alcoholism that provides a better explanation than we have had previously.

When anthropologists first began to focus on the cultural context of drinking, they emphasized that understanding such behaviors could be explained within the terms and realities of the specific culture under study. This was the primary reason behind Malinowski's development in 1944 of a functional description of culture. Radcliffe-Brown's subsequent refinement in 1952 of the functional description of culture focused on the interrelated and interconnected nature of the social system rather than the satisfaction of biological drives. His structural-functional description still sought to operate and explain cultural systems within the framework of their own contexts (Jarvie 1968). This theoretical and methodological construction provided a very important basis for the description of cultures throughout the first half of the twentieth century and is still an important consideration in most anthropological work (Manners and Kaplan 1968). Anthropologists first began to describe drinking practices in much the same way (Mandelbaum 1965, Heath 1975, Marshall 1980).

Functional and structural-functional explanations do not generate the dogmatic adherence in modern anthropology that they possessed in the past, but they are still important aspects of adaptation. Certain beliefs, behaviors, and energetic exchanges are adaptive because they perpetuate the viable, cultural structures that are necessary for the continued existence of the individual, the group, and the species. When the ideas or activities of certain groups do not meet these adaptive criteria or become maladaptive and go uncorrected, then the extinction of that particular cultural system becomes possible, and sometimes likely (Turnbull 1972).

Anthropologists who initially contributed to the worldwide, crosscultural data base concerning the use of alcoholic beverages were not specifically engaged in alcohol studies. However, it is a credit to anthropological descriptions based on the concepts of culture, structure, function, and adaptation that it became so readily apparent to investigators that the use of alcoholic beverages was prevalent in human cultural systems and that alcohol was frequently important in the context of ritual, ceremonial, and social life. These investigators concluded that the use of alcoholic beverages commonly functioned within the structure of specific, traditional cultural systems. Although some cultures regarded alcohol negatively, they generally found that alcoholic beverages initiated and maintained important ceremonial and social relationships within and between groups. Furthermore, they found that alcohol problems, alcoholism, and addiction per se were rare, if not nonexistent among small, traditional societies (Heath 1983).

The absence of alcoholism or addiction among the small, usually self-contained cultures that had been the traditional target of anthropological investigations was the first major contribution to the study of alcohol problems in complex societies.

Anthropologists were unable to obtain data suggesting that societies that exhibited more traditional patterns of social organization were also likely victims of alcoholism and addiction (Service 1962). Unless we are to conclude that many different anthropologists from many different personal, cultural, and academic backgrounds were all in error, we must consider the validity of this apparent fact.

Room (1984) has suggested that anthropologists have engaged an ethnographic bias of functionalism and an ethnocentric bias of a group of individuals enculturated into a system that puts a high value on the use of alcoholic beverages in order to conclude that alcoholism and addiction per se do not occur in traditional societies. Although the accusation of an ethnocentric bias is probably far too broad, the experience of subjects in this study would seem to suggest that at least American culture is one that assigns a high positive value on the drinking of alcoholic beverages. The same is true for the accusation of an ethnographic bias in the application of functional explanations of the relationship of alcohol to the individual and culture. Although the concept of function is critically valuable to the concept of adaptation, anthropology has not engaged in simplistic functional analysis for quite some time. Anthropology pays close attention to function because that is often the way things work.

If we can develop a better anthropological theory of alcoholism, then it may be possible to re-examine previous studies in order to discover to what extent anthropologists may have overlooked important data. At the moment, it would seem prudent to accept the conclusions of so many competent ethnographers and seek an explanation for the development of alcoholism that can also account for the apparent lack of alcohol problems in small, traditional societies.

A productive theory of alcoholism would then begin with the assumption that the use of alcoholic beverages is functional and adaptive at less complex levels of sociocultural integration. This is not to say that alcoholism is a relatively new development. We have historical evidence that suggests that drunkenness and habitual drunkenness were both significant problems in antiquity. Examples from ancient Egyptian hieroglyphics, Sumerian cuneiform, and Indian and Roman texts (Mandelbaum 1965) all indicate that the use of alcoholic beverages was problematic for some individuals and for society. However, all these references to drunkenness that imply the possibility of alcoholism in antiquity appear in the context of state level social organization.

Ethnohistoric evidence concerning problems associated with alcohol use would seem to support this proposal. The high incidence of alcohol problems observed among individuals of traditional societies seems only to occur as they experience acculturation into systems that exhibit more complex, state level social organization. MacAndrew and Edgerton (1969) demonstrated through such ethnohistorical data that drunken comportment was learned behavior rather than the result of the pharmacological properties of alcohol. Leland (1976) showed that the firewater myth that had been applied to many Native Americans was not an accurate description of the cause of the high incidence of alcoholism in these populations. Hill (1984) used ethnohistorical data to review heavy drinking in the context of acculturation. He noted that explanatory models have generally focused on drinking as (1) a response to sociocultural disorganization, (2) a response to deprivation, and (3) an expression of traditional beliefs and practices. None of these works suggest that alcoholism was an indigenous problem before culture contact was sustained.

However, increasing levels of sociocultural integration cannot be the only cause of alcoholism. If this were the case, we could expect virtually every member in complex societies and all those who sustained significant contact with such cultures to experience alcohol problems. Also, the use of alcoholic beverages appears to be adaptive for most individuals in complex societies. Gordon (1984) clearly demonstrates that alcohol use is frequently more asocial and pathological as economies around the world become more fully cash-based, but that it continues to promote social and economic integration as part of the process of adaptation. Studies of bars, modernization, and urban drinking contexts suggest that there can be many economic and social benefits of using alcoholic beverages. But here again, no one has suggested that traditional practices, even when they involve heavy drinking, lead to alcoholism, except in the context of acculturation.

The data generated by this study of members of Alcoholics Anonymous cannot directly address problems of acculturation, but they can address the development of alcoholism within the context of American society and suggest possible explanations that also could be of use in studies of culture contact. The use of alcohol is functional and adaptive for many, if not most individuals in American society. Since it seems that alcoholism is essentially a condition that only occurs at higher levels of sociocultural integration, we need to be able to specify possible mechanisms that could be responsible for the obviously maladaptive aspects that alcohol presents to some individuals.

The first such mechanism that should be considered is the possibility that there is some biogenetic predisposition for some people to develop alcoholism. There has been no success in the effort to identify an alcoholic gene, or specify any particular metabolic differences that could contribute to the development of alcoholism (Vaillant). However, data from studies of twins strongly suggests there is some genetic basis for differences in drinking frequency and quantity (Goodwin 1983).

Many members of Alcoholics Anonymous claim that alcohol simply affected them more acutely than others they observed during the course of their drinking. Many said that from the first time they drank alcohol, they lost all control over the amount they drank. They simply wanted more. Most AA members claim that they never drank to be social, but drank to get drunk. They drank because they liked the effect. They drank quickly and massively to achieve the state of intoxication that they desire.

William Madsen's *The American Alcoholic: The Nature-Nurture Controversy in Alcoholic Research and Therapy* (1974) is the only previous anthropological work that includes long-term observation of AA members. From his observational study and from the synthesis of scientific investigations at that time, he concluded that most true alcoholics seem to have some biological predisposition to alcoholism. Although much of the speculation in which he engaged has been put to rest, the general conclusion still seems to reflect the experience of AA members in this study. Madsen carefully differentiates between the "primary" alcoholic who is characterized by daily drinking early in the development of the condition and the periodic drinker who does not become a daily drinker until late in the development of the syndrome. This type of "secondary" alcoholic is characterized as a heavy social drinker who finally steps over the line through some process of habituation. The primary alcoholic is considered to be more likely the result of genetic factors and the secondary more likely a product of the environment. Both types were represented in this study of AA members, but the distinction between those who inherit alcoholism and those who learn to be alcoholics is not so clear.

While many members, due to their perception of the way that alcohol affected them, claim that they were born alcoholics, they also claim to have learned to practice alcoholism. Conversely, most AA members who claimed to have slowly, almost imperceptibly developed a dependence on alcohol also claim to have been affected qualitatively and differently than normal people when drinking. Obviously, there may be some biogenetic predisposition to the development of alcoholism, but most members in this study seem to think that anyone can become an alcoholic. If any individual drinks long enough and hard enough, they probably risk developing a dependence on alcohol.

Madsen's work was appropriately received in the interdisciplinary field of alcohol studies, although it was overlooked for the most part by anthropologists. He made the point that alcoholism is probably inherited *and* learned and that it exhibited substantial variation in etiology, development, and symptomology. Most importantly, he recognized that the *anxious American cultural milieu* was a critical factor in the cause and practice of alcoholism, and he suggested that the problem must be approached from the holistic perspective that is so highly touted by anthropologists. As many others had done before and have continued to do, he cautioned that true alcoholics had to be differentiated from problem drinkers and treated appropriately. He suggested that simplistic answers to the complex biological, psychological, social, and cultural factors that caused alcoholism would probably not be forthcoming. And they have not.

While the complexity of alcohol dependence cannot be denied, it should still be the goal of science to offer some general explanation of alcoholism that would be helpful to health care professionals and lay persons alike. Many models that assist in the diagnosis and treatment of the alcoholic have been offered. An anthropological model should also be of similar value, but the most productive model would be one that might prevent the development of alcoholism. Such a model would also provide an adequate explanation of the recovery process and help in the prevention of alcohol abuse by problem drinkers. The benefit of such a model to recovering alcoholics and others in American society and to countless, suffering individuals would be enormous.

In short, we need to know why some people drink to destructive extremes, given the same opportunity and conditions that present few problems to the majority of those who drink alcoholic beverages. It does not seem that all individuals who may have a genetic predisposition to alcoholism actually develop a problem. Some people may recognize the lack of control, experience blackouts, and reasonably conclude that they don't like drinking. Others may recognize that alcohol affects them substantially more than it does other people, and although they may drink socially on a sporadic basis, they do not drink habitually, nor do they develop a dependence on alcohol. In order to determine some systematic causal mechanism, it may be helpful to review the hypothetical reasons why people drink, which have been offered by anthropological investigators, and compare these to the data gathered from subjects in this study.

Horton (1943) suggested that people tended to drink more to drunkenness due to subsistence anxiety. Through a broad-based crosscultural comparison using the Human Relations Area Files at Yale University, he found a direct correlation between the lack of prediction concerning subsistence supplies and drinking to drunkenness. He concluded that in all cultures people tend to drink to relieve anxiety. Members of Alcoholics Anonymous cite anxiety over a wide range of issues as some of the reasons why they drank. Some anxieties were related to jobs, financial worries, and material aspirations. However, they also cited anxieties over relations with families, friends, co-workers, business and professional associates as reasons why they drank. In addition, they said that they suffered from anxieties concerning their own self-worth and self-image. So there seems to be some support for Horton's hypothesis among members of Alcoholics Anonymous, but anxiety or fear appears to be only one of a class of reasons over which they drank. Many normal people deal with considerable anxiety without drinking to drunkenness.

Peter Field (1962) re-examined Horton's data and came to a much different conclusion. His work suggested that anxiety was not the best predictor of drinking to drunkenness across cultures. He found that cultures that lacked corporate kinship structures were the most likely to foster drunkenness. Highly formalized duties and responsibilities to kin constituted effective social controls over individualized behaviors and precluded drunkenness. Although alcohol was used, its use was rigidly restricted to the proper ritual, ceremonial, and social contexts. The stories of AA members reflect experiences in which broken family structures are accorded a causal relationship to both the onset of heavy drinking and the development of alcohol dependence. However, given the virtual absence of any formalized, corporate kinship structures in mainstream American culture and the significant absence of any formalized prescriptions regarding duties and responsibilities to kin, this hypothesis hardly seems an appropriate explanation for the development of alcoholism. If it were, the United States would be in serious difficulty and we could expect an incidence of heavy drinking that would include almost everyone. Considering the exceedingly weak family structure of the highly mobile, affluent, and mostly serially monogamous middle class, and the troubled family structure of some groups of the lower class, America would be almost totally alcoholic. Obviously, this is not the case.

Klausner (1964) hypothesized a negative relationship between drunkenness in a secular setting in cultures that had a high symbolic value on blood in sacred contexts. His sample of data and methods have been criticized (Bacon 1981), although there is some reason to believe that the sacred, symbolic use of alcohol in some cultures might mitigate against drunkenness in a secular setting (Bales 1944). The only subjects in this study to have experienced any such sacred, symbolic use of alcohol were Catholics, who seem to have been unaffected by ritual associations in the development of alcohol dependence. However, it is important to note that about one third of the adult population in the United States does not consume alcohol. A large proportion of these people cite religious beliefs as a primary reason for their abstinence. For them, it would seem that any use of alcoholic beverages has a negative, symbolic value relative to their perception of the sacred. Given these facts and the prevalence of alcohol use in secular settings, this would not seem to be a good explanation for the development of alcoholism.

McClelland and colleagues (1972) proposed a hypothetical relationship between cultures that did not institutionalize maleness and heavy drinking. Through the study of folktales from a selection of cultures, they suggested that in cultures that did not formally codify maleness, men were much more likely to drink to drunkenness in order to feel more powerful. This "power" hypothesis has some relationship to the reasons why some members of AA said they drank. Many members said that one of the effects they relished the most about alcohol intoxication was the feeling of power that it induced. It was great "to feel ten feet tall and bullet proof." While this brute, physical sense of power was most often cited by men, women indicated that although alcohol did not produce this particular effect, other enhancements to personal power were perceived. Women often referred to feelings of sexual power, which were intensified by intoxication. Even though many members expressed the perceived enhancement of personal power through intoxication, it does not appear to be a good explanation for the development of alcohol dependence among the members of Alcoholics Anonymous in this study.

Bacon and colleagues (1965) first offered a dependency-conflict theory that could be used to understand why people drink. Bacon (1974,1981) refined this hypothesis and suggested that drinking to drunkenness is often the result of a conflict between dependence and independence. This theory predicts that drinking to drunkenness will be more prevalent in cultures where childhood indulgence gives way to significant pressures toward self-reliance, achievement, and independence in adulthood. As Bacon states:

Insobriety is conceived to be associated with a type of dependence-independence conflict. In this context, dependence refers to a behavioral complex related to seeking for help which is universally acquired in the course of normal development. As a consequence of this universal experience, every child develops an elaborate repertoire of help-seeking sequences of behavior. As the child grows older the help giving behavior of adults is modified in response to the developing capabilities of the child and the expectations of the society with regard to autonomy. . . . Since the human animal lives in groups and no individual is entirely self-sufficient, the need to seek help persists in varying degrees throughout life. While the necessity of asking for help is less obvious in adulthood than in infancy, it is nevertheless present universally. This point should be emphasized because in many groups in our own society behavior which is labeled "independent" is highly valued and help-seeking behavior is considered childish and unbecoming in an adult, especially in an adult male. (Bacon 1981: 768–769)

American society is obviously one with significant conflict of this type and many members of Alcoholics Anonymous in this study specified this conflict as not only a major reason for their drinking, but a primary reason for the denial of alcoholism and later one of the reasons for difficulties in recovery.

The theories that have been developed by anthropologists all have some practical utility as reasons for drinking to drunkenness by alcoholics in AA. However, the hypotheses that anxiety, social control, secular versus sacred settings, or the need for power have important predictive value do not seem to reflect the experience of subjects in this study. Although these motivations for drunkenness were cited as important factors for bouts of drinking by members of AA, they considered such reasons more properly "good excuses" for drinking rather than causes of their alcohol dependence.

Dependency-conflict theory does reflect important aspects of what many members referred to as "alcoholic thinking." Most said that pressures to achieve to a certain level of expectation and the failure to do so were critical to the development of their alcoholism. Importantly, dependency-conflict theory demonstrates that there is a relationship between idealized cultural values, which are practically impossible to realize, and drunkenness. Yet it does not address why only some of the people in our culture develop alcoholism or problems related to alcohol abuse. If we can assume that most individuals in American society are subjected to the same conflict regarding idealized versus practical behavior, then we need to be able to understand why only a small proportion of individuals becomes alcohol dependent as a result of such conflicts.

Gregory Bateson (1971) proposed a theory of alcoholism that was published in the *Journal of Psychiatry*. Although this work had an important impact in alcohol studies and contributed significantly to the construction of a developmental model of alcoholism and recovery (Brown 1985), it has been virtually buried and remains obscure in anthropology. Bateson suggested that the alcoholic, when sober, is engaged in life on the basis of an epistemological error. He suggested that this fundamental error in understanding and knowing the world as it really exists actually seems conventional and is readily accepted in the context of western culture, but it is unacceptable in the context of systems theory. In an effort to apply systems theory to the problem of alcoholism, Bateson presumed that the causes of alcohol dependence could be found in the sober state of the alcoholic. If the sober state of alcoholics compelled them to drink, then whatever motivated them in sobriety could not be expected to assist in the reduction or control of alcohol dependence. He also suggested that if there was something inherently wrong with the alcoholic's style of sobriety that drove one to drink, then intoxication must present some type of subjective correction of the error.

Virtually all members of Alcoholics Anonymous in this study claimed to have always had an underlying sense of separation from others. Separation was manifest in their shyness, anxiety, or insecurity in relation to others. Alcohol intoxication "fixed all that." When they began to use alcohol, it appeared that they had found the perfect "social lubricant." Alcohol made everything all right. They became an integral part of the social environment. But AA members said that eventually "alcohol quit working." As they tried to recapture the "reality" that intoxication afforded them at first, they drifted deeper into the cycle of despair so characteristic of alcoholism.

Bateson suggested that the alcoholic has an exaggerated sense of self and personal power, which is strongly reinforced by the system of beliefs encouraged in American society. He also suggested that beliefs define and constrain individuals' perceptions and actions. This is precisely the situation that AA members describe as "alcoholic thinking." They said that what they "believed" determined their perception of the world and their relation to others. Bateson said that this erroneous epistemology was based "on a body of habitual assumptions or premises implicit in the relationship of man and environment, and that these premises may be true or false" (Bateson 1971: 4). Goodenough (1992) makes this same point regarding the capacity for beliefs, and Kearney (1976) concerning world view.

Obviously, our beliefs do not need to be correct in order for us to believe them. Our world view need not be accurate for us to act accordingly. We simply need a set of propositions that can lead to a commitment to action. Within the context of culture and individual human activities, the ultimate judge of the appropriateness of the belief system for us is the extent to which specific behaviors are *perceived* to be adaptive or maladaptive. Once again, given the short life-span of human beings, these perceptions do not always need to be true to be believed.

Members of AA said that they operated their lives based on false premises, but they only recognized the error after they began to recover from alcoholism, after they began to transform *the sober state*. Before they surrendered to a power greater than themselves and admitted their basic dependence as mere human beings, they believed those false premises and behaved accordingly. Through the language of Alcoholics Anonymous, they gradually came to believe in a new set of propositions, transformed their view of the world, and founded a new basis for action.

The fundamental error of "alcoholic thinking" or an "alcoholic epistemology" is the perception of the self as an autonomous, independent source of power within the universe, one that is truly capable of controlling existence. Subjects of this study identified this fundamental error as the essential *cause* of their alcoholism. This constitutes strong support for Bateson's hypothesis. Bacon emphasized that dependence on other human beings is a universal fact of life and Radcliffe-Brown suggested that human beings are even dependent on other mysterious forces that are beyond our meager human comprehension. Idealized cultural beliefs that fail to properly acknowledge these facts reinforce an error in the very nature of knowledge and understanding. It is our interconnectedness that makes us a part of our families, a part of our cultures, a part of the human species, a part of the planet on which we have evolved, and a part of the universe that we believe mysteriously came into existence over 15 billion years ago. We are not alone.

Past anthropological work concerning the use and abuse of alcohol by human beings and the results of this study suggest the following facts:

1. Alcohol use appears to be predominantly functional and adaptive, especially but not exclusively, at less complex levels of sociocultural integration.
2. Most behavioral problems associated with alcohol, particularly alcoholism, seem to occur

only in the context of, or in conjunction with, cultures that operate at the state level of social organization.

3. Drinking to drunkenness seems to predictably occur with greater frequency as a response to dependence-independence conflicts involving cultural beliefs and behaviors. Anxiety, fear, lack of structural, symbolic, or social controls, and needs to enhance personal power are probably subsumed within dependency-conflict.

4. This and other ethnographic analyses of Alcoholics Anonymous suggest that although complex biological, psychological, social, and cultural factors generate extreme variation in the onset, development, practice, symptomology, and recovery of alcoholics, there is evidence to conclude that the primary underlying cause of alcoholism in the United States is an epistemological error in the individual alcoholic. The fundamental quality of this error concerns the nature of the self, the nature of the relation of the self to others, and the nature of existence in this world.

Clearly, such a bold statement is not intended to suggest that a simple answer to the problem of alcoholism is now at hand. However, these propositions can provide the foundation for a somewhat more complete level of explanation of alcoholism within the context of our current knowledge. All these premises seem to be well documented through anthropological and other investigations. Presently, only the final hypothesis would seem to be critically problematic. However, it is necessary to resolve such uncertainties if a truly productive anthropological theory of alcoholism is to be fully realized.

Bateson's work in developing a theory of alcoholism was based on his study of the premises of alcoholism as it was understood at the time, the premises of the AA system of treating it, and the premises of the organization of Alcoholics Anonymous. He also worked intensively for two years with a small sample of alcoholics in the veteran's hospital in Palo Alto, California. The theory he developed is strongly supported by Madsen's observational study of Alcoholics Anonymous in which he participated in meetings, developed an ongoing seminar that AA members attended to discuss various aspects of alcoholism and recovery, and participated in 12-step calls and social activities typical of the AA community. While much of Madsen's work centered on members' stories and is necessarily anecdotal, the long-term nature of his observations suggest that they are significant.

The long-term observational study of participation in Alcoholics Anonymous and the description that has been presented here has specifically demonstrated the validity of Bateson's theory of alcoholism. Subjects in this study referred to the epistemological error that was described by Bateson as "alcoholic thinking." Their conclusions concerning the necessity of "getting rid of alcoholic thinking" and changing their entire system of believing and world view are in accord and constitute strong support for the theory.

There is also a great deal of support for the theory in much of the work that has been done in medicine, psychology, and sociology. Levin (1987) and Denzin (1987) used the concept of alcoholism as a form of self-pathology to describe the nature of alcoholism and suggest treatment appropriate to this model. Brown (1985) based her developmental model of alcoholism and recovery, in large part, on Bateson's theory. Her study also provided strong support for the theory as an accurate reflection of the experience of AA members. However, to a great extent these models focus on the treatment of alcoholism and do not address the issues with which anthropology is typically concerned.

One of the most critical explanations of anthropological significance concerns how such an epistemological error could be accounted for in terms of evolution and adaptation. Anthropology needs to know why some individuals are afflicted in such a mistaken manner and others seem to be unaffected. Psychological explanations are often not particularly satisfying to anthropology. Anthropologists want to know what might be the cultural, adaptive, and/or evolutionary mechanisms that may be operating in the process.

At first glance, it is difficult to see how a productive theory can be generated on the basis of such a class of individual exceptions. Therefore, perhaps we are approaching the whole problem backward. Perhaps alcoholics and their apparent epistemological malfunctions are not such clear exceptions and malfunctions at all. As anthropologists, we know that one of the most important facts of human life is that no human being exists in isolation. We are always a part of some group, some culture. We exist within interrelated aggregations of individuals. We also know that such aggregations can be highly variable, but they always appear to be systems that are propelled to perpetuate themselves through the structural sharing of language, beliefs, and behaviors. In order to remain viable, particularly in an evolutionary sense, individuals are compelled through enculturation into systems that coerce the individual to accept and respond to various duties and responsibilities in relation to others.

However, as anthropologists we also know that adaptation and evolution occur through the mechanism of variation. Cookie cutter cultures that simply kept stamping out the same individuals without the possibility of human behavioral variation could not adapt to changing conditions and could not endure. Nor could a species without biological variation be expected to last any time at all on the evolutionary scale. Therefore, the most reasonable explanation would be that the structure of the human mind is such that we perceive all too well that we are trapped in our own bodies and are separate from others in this very important sense. All human beings are capable of recognizing that the self is unique and apart from others (Kearney 1984). We can see how this could be extremely important and advantageous in creating the likelihood of innovation, new and novel ideas about the world, and how it could be manipulated and exploited to the benefit of the individual, the family, and the culture. The generation of novel behaviors is analogous to the generation of a novel utterance in human language. Without this capability, there would be no true language, true culture, or true humanity. In short, all human beings probably have the tendency to operationalize such an epistemological error and become what would normally be considered selfish and self-absorbed. Evolutionary biology informs us that this is not always a bad thing.

If all human beings are capable of operating with this epistemological error and if alcohol has the capability to subjectively correct this error, then it is extremely easy to see how alcohol use is so functional and so adaptive in less complex, traditional cultures. Alcohol and intoxication correct the error. It enhances the sense of ritual, ceremonial, and social dependencies and re-establishes reality *connected to the other*. In primitive and traditional culture, structural mechanisms such as egalitarian ideology, reciprocity, the symbolic structure of ritual, and kinship systems strongly reinforce this reality. In such a social environment, the addictive use of alcohol is generally unnecessary and a lack of alcoholism or addiction has been observed. But, once individuals and groups are faced with the exigencies of life at the state level of social organization, they are confronted with the de-personalization of their existence. As they struggle with the resulting alienation, they are more likely to operationalize the epistemological error. Egalitarian ideas and the concept of reciprocity no longer have the same meaning. The symbolic structure of ritual and kinship undergoes transformation and loses its ability to reinforce the reality of interdependence and being intmately connected to one another. Politically, this degeneration of traditional togetherness assists the state in replacing traditional social control with political control. The structure of human relations is transformed, and the knowledge and understanding of the self and the other becomes more differentiated. The cultural context of the state fosters the operationalization of the epistemological error. Through language and through the transformation of the belief system, different behaviors are encouraged, and the individual becomes even more alienated and alone.

Since such a recognition and perception of the distinction between the self and the other is probably due to the evolutionary advantage provided by variation and the resulting innovation that may be adaptive, we can account for the fact that only some individuals suffer from alcoholism. Within the context of such adaptive variation, we can assume that individuals who become alcohol dependent perhaps experience the sense of isolation on a deeper level. For such individuals, alcohol may provide deeply needed correction of an error initially generated by cultural belief, but sustained by personal fear and habituation. Some people probably have a greater tendency to perceive the duality of the self and the other. We may also consider the possibility that alcohol intoxication is only a single solution in the attempt to correct the epistemological error. Other addictive behaviors may also result from this same mechanism.

Modern American culture has been characterized as an addictive society (Imbach 1992). The level of alienation, the estrangement and loneliness of millions of individual human beings who have no sense of connectedness and little sense of really belonging with others, has risen to a critical and dramatic state. Alcohol may be the most prevalent "antidote" to correct this mistaken perception of the relation between ourselves and everything around us, but other attempts and addictions abound. Other drugs, cigarettes, and coffee (which are also drugs), and food are substances that are used in an effort to correct the error. Sex, jogging, and exercise are activities in which people engage addictively in order to enhance self-image and correct the error. The acquisition of greater material wealth is pursued in order to correct the error. Politicians don't want the error corrected. They engage in everything they can to convince the population that we are all impotent individuals and it is you against her, him against me, and us against them.

BUT FOR THE GRACE OF GOD

Members of Alcoholics Anonymous claim that the compulsion to drink is removed after they begin to change their way of thinking and believing. They claim that they are able to accomplish this change only through the development of a spiritual or conceptual awareness. They no longer have the compulsion to drink because they no longer need to correct the error. It has ceased operation. They believe that to exist as a human being is to exist in interdependence and interconnection with others and with everything, not in the isolation of the self. The practical expression of what they call spiritual awareness is essentially the practice of the concern for the other and acceptance of their limitations as mere human beings.

During the course of this study, many members said that as a result of their alcoholic thinking they either did not know, or had forgotten, how to love before they came to the program of Alcoholics Anonymous. At a meeting one Saturday morning, a woman in her fifties who had been sober for over nine years and recently diagnosed with cancer said, "I had always heard the saying, 'God is love,' but I never really thought that meant anything to me, but the other day I heard someone say, 'Love is God,' and you know, I thought that's what it is. Love is God." She began to quietly weep before she continued, "That's what the AA program has really taught me—How to Love."

For this woman and many others in AA, the correction of the error is made through the recovery of love. Love by its very nature is concerned for the other. It is not boastful nor selfish. It does not insist on its own way. Alcoholics Anonymous teaches us that to really live this life—faith, hope, and love must remain and endure. But the greatest of these is Love.

Bibliography

Ablon, Joan. 1984. Family Research and Alcoholism. In *Recent Developments in Alcoholism*, Vol. 2, edited by M. Galanter. New York: Plenum Press, pp. 383–396.

Agar, Michael. 1984. Comment on Room's Alcohol and Ethnography: A Case of Problem Deflation? *Current Anthropology* 25:169–176, 178.

———. 1986. *Speaking of Ethnography: Qualitative Research Methods Series 2*. Beverly Hills, Calif.: Sage.

Albaugh, Bernard J., and Phillipo Anderson. 1974. Peyote in the Treatment of Alcoholism among the American Indians. *American Journal of Psychiatry* 131:1247–1250.

Alcoholics Anonymous. 1939. *Alcoholics Anonymous*. First edition. New York: Alcoholics Anonymous.

———. 1947. *AA Grapevine*. New York. AA Grapevine.

———. 1957. *AA Comes of Age*. New York: Alcoholics Anonymous.

———. 1967. *As Bill Sees It: The AA Way of Life*. New York: Alcoholics Anonymous World Services.

———. 1976. *Alcoholics Anonymous*. Third edition. New York: Alcoholics Anonymous World Services.

———. 1980. *Dr. Bob and the Good Oldtimers: A Biography with Recollections of Early AA in the Midwest*. New York: Alcoholics Anonymous World Services.

———.1981. *The Twelve Steps and the Twelve Traditions*. New York: Alcoholics Anonymous World Services.

———. 1984. *Pass It On: The Story of Bill Wilson and How the AA Message Reached the World*. New York: Alcoholics Anonymous World Services.

Allchin, F. R. 1979. India: The Ancient Home of Distillation? *Man* 14:55–63.

Anderson, Barbara Galatin. 1979. How French Children Learn to Drink. In *Beliefs, Behaviors and Alcoholic Beverages: A Cross Cultural Survey*, edited by M. Marshall. Ann Arbor: University of Michigan Press, pp. 429-432.

Antze, Paul. 1987. Symbolic Action in Alcoholics Anonymous. In *Constructive Drinking: Perspectives on Drink from Anthropology*, edited by M. Douglas. New York: Cambridge University Press, pp. 149–181.

Armor, D. J., J. M. Polich, and H. B. Stanbul. 1976. *Alcohol and Treatment*. Santa Monica: Rand Corporation.

Atkins, C. K. 1987. Alcoholic Beverage Advertising: Its Context and Impact. In *Control*

Issues in Alcohol Abuse Prevention: Strategies for States and Communities. Advances in Substance Abuse, Supplement 1. Greenwich, Conn: JAI Press, pp. 267–287.

Babor, Thomas F., and Richard J. Lauerman. 1986. Classification and Forms of Inebriety: Historical Antecedents of Alcoholic Typologies. In *Recent Developments in Alcoholism,* Vol. 4, edited by M. Galanter. New York: Plenum Press, pp. 113–144.

Bacon, M. K., H. Barry III, and I. L. Child. 1965. A Cross-Cultural Study of Drinking: Relations to Other Features of Culture. *Quarterly Journal of Studies on Alcohol.* Supplement 3, Vol. 26, pp. 29–48.

Bacon, Margaret K. 1974. The Dependency-Conflict Hypothesis and the Frequency of Drunkenness: Further Evidence from a Cross-Cultural Study. *Quarterly Journal of Studies of Alcohol* 35:863–876.

————.1981. Cross-Cultural Perspectives on Motivations for Drinking. In *Handbook of Cross-Cultural Development,* edited by R. H. Munroe, R. L. Munroe, and B. B. Whiting. New York: Garland STPM Press, pp. 755–782.

Baekeland, Fredrick, Lawrence Lundwall, and Benjamin Kissin. 1975. Methods for the Treatment of Chronic Alcoholism: A Critical Appraisal. In *Research Advances in Alcohol and Drug Problems*, Vol . 2, edited by Gibbons et al. New York: John Wiley and Sons, pp. 247–328.

Baker, S., B. O'Neil, and R. Karpf. 1984. *Injury Facts Book.* Lexington, Mass.: Heath.

Bales, R. F. 1944. The Therapeutic Role of Alcoholics Anonymous As Seen by a Sociologist. *Quarterly Journal of Studies on Alcohol* 5:267–278.

Barnes, Grace M. 1977. The Development of Adolescent Drinking Behavior: An Evaluative Review of the Impact of the Socialization Process within the Family. *Adolescence* 12:571–591.

Bateson, Gregory. 1971. The Cybernetics of Self: A Theory of Alcoholism. *Psychiatry* 34:1–18.

Bean, M. 1975. Alcoholics Anonymous II. *Psychiatric Annals* 5:7–57.

Bennett, Linda A. 1984a. Contributions from Anthropology to the Study of Alcoholism. In *Recent Developments in Alcoholism,* Vol. 2, edited by M. Galanter. New York: Plenum Press, pp. 303–338.

————.1984b. Comment on Room's Alcohol and Ethnography: A Case of Problem Deflation. *Current Anthropology* 25:178.

Bernard, H. Russell. 1988. *Research Methods in Cultural Anthropology.* Beverly Hills, Calif.: Sage.

Bernard, R., P. Killworth, D. Kroenfeld, and L. Sailer. 1984. The Problem of Informant Accuracy: The Validity of Retrospective. In *Annual Review of Anthropology,* Vol. 13, edited by Siegel et al. Palo Alto, Calif.: Annual Reviews, pp. 495–518.

Berreman, Gerald D. 1956. Drinking patterns of the Aleut. *Quarterly Journal of Studies on Alcohol* 17:502–514.

Bissell, LeClair, and Paul W. Haberman. 1984. *Alcoholism in the Professions.* New York: Oxford University Press.

Blane, H. T. 1978. Half a Bottle Is Better Than None. *Contemporary Psychology* 23:396–397.

Bourne, P. G. and R. Fox, eds. 1973. *Alcoholism: Progress in Research and Treatment.* New York: Academic Press.

Brandsma, J. M., M. C. Maultsby, Jr., and R. J. Welsh. 1980. *Outpatient Treatment of Alcoholism: A Review and Comparative Study.* Baltimore: University Park Press.

Brown, Stephanie. 1985. *Treating the Alcoholic: A Developmental Model of Recovery.* New York: John Wiley and Sons.

Bunzel, Ruth. 1940. The Role of Alcohol in Two Central American Communities. *Psychiatry* 3:361–383.

Cahalan, Don. 1970. *Problem Drinking: A National Survey.* San Fransisco: Jossey-Bass.

Cahalan, Don, ed. 1969. *American Drinking Practices: A National Study of Drinking Behavior and Attitudes.* Monograph no. 6. New Brunswick, N.J.: Rutgers Center of Alcohol Studies.

Chalmers, D. K. 1979. The Alcoholic's Controlled Drinking Time. *World Alcohol Project* 1:18–27.

Child, I. L., M. K. Bacon, and H. Barry III. 1965. A Cross-Cutural Study of Drinking: Descriptive Measurements of Drinking Customs. *Quarterly Journal of Studies on Alcohol.* Supplement 3, Vol. 26, pp.1–28.

Chrouser, Kelly Renee. 1990. *A Critical Analysis of the Discourse and Reconstructed Stories Shared by Recovering Female Alcoholics in Alcoholics Anonymous.* Unpublished Ph.D. diss. University of Nebraska, Speech and Dramatic Art.

Cohen, F. G., R. D. Walker, and S. Stanley. 1981. The Role of Anthropology in Interdisciplinary Research on Indian Alcoholism and Treatment Outcome. *Journal of Studies on Alcohol* 42:819–821.

Colliver, J. D., and H. Malin. 1986. State and National Trends in Alcohol Related Mortality: 1975–1982. *Alcohol Health and Research World* 10:60–64.

Collman, Jeff. 1979. Social Order and the Exchange of Liquor: A Theory of Drinking Among Australian Aborigines. *Journal of Anthropological Research* 35:208–224.

Cox, W. Miles, ed. 1987. *Treatment and Prevention of Alcohol Problems: A Resource Manual.* Orlando: Academic Press.

Csordas, Thomas J. 1988. Elements of Charismatic Persuasion and Healing. *Medical Anthropology Quarterly New Series* 2:121–142.

Davies, D. L. 1962. Normal Drinking in Recovered Alcohol Addicts. *Quarterly Journal of Studies on Alcohol* 23:94–104.

———. 1976. Definitional Issues in Alcoholism: Interdisciplinary Approaches to an Enduring Problem. In *An Interdisciplinary Approach to Alcoholism,* edited by Tarter and Sugarman. Reading, Mass.: Addison-Wesley.

Denzin, Norman K. 1977. Notes on the Criminogenic Hypothesis: A Case Study of the American Liquor Industry. *American Sociological Review* 42:905–920.

———. 1987. *The Alcoholic Self.* Beverly Hills, Calif.: Sage.

Ditman, K. S., G. G. Crawford, E. W. Forgy, H. Moskowitz, and C. MacAndrew. 1967. A Controlled Experiment on the Use of Court Probation for Drunk Arrests. *American Journal of Psychiatry* 124:160–163.

Douglas, Mary. 1987. *Constructive Drinking: Perspectives on Drink from Anthropology.* New York: Cambridge University Press.

Edwards, G. 1982. *The Treatment of Drinking Problems: A Guide for the Helping Professions.* New York: McGraw-Hill.

Emrick, Chad D. 1989a. Alcoholics Anonymous: Emerging Concepts (Overview). In *Recent Developments in Alcoholism,* Vol. 7, edited by M. Galanter. New York: Plenum Press, pp. 3–10.

———. 1989b. Alcoholics Anonymous Membership Characteristics and Effectiveness as Treatment. In *Recent Developments in Alcoholism,* Vol. 7, edited by M. Galanter. New York: Plenum Press, pp. 37–53.

Emrick, Chad D., C. L. Lassic, and M. Edwards. 1977. Non-professional Peers as Therapeutic Agent. In *Effective Psychotherapy: A Handbook of Research,* edited by A. S. Gurman and A. M. Razim. New York: Pergamon Press.

Estroff, S., W. S. Lachiotte, L. C. Illingworth, and A. Johnston. 1991. Everybody's Got a

Little Mental Illness: Accounts of Illness and Self Among People with Severe, Persistent Mental Illness. *Medical Anthropology Quarterly New Series* 5:300–330.

Everett, M. W., J. O. Waddell, D. B. Heath, eds. 1976. *Cross Cultural Approaches to the Study of Alcohol: An Interdisciplinary Perspective.* The Hague: Mouton Publishers.

Field, Peter. 1962. A New Cross Cultural Study of Drunkenness. In *Society, Culture, and Drinking*, edited by D. Pittman and C. R. Snyder. New York: John Wiley and Sons.

Finney, John W. and Rudolf H. Moos. 1991. The Long Term Course of Treated Alcoholism: Mortality, Relapse, and Remission Rates and Comparisons and Community Controls. *Quarterly Journal of Alcoholism* 52:44–54.

Galanter, Marc A. 1983. Religious Influence and the Etiology of Substance Abuse. In *Etiologic Aspects of Alcohol and Drug Abuse*, edited by Gottheil et al. Springfield, Ill.: Charles C. Thomas, pp 238–248.

Galanter, Marc A., ed. 1983–1990. *Recent Developments in Alcoholism,* Vols. 1–8. New York: Plenum Press.

Gallant, Donald M. 1987. *Alcoholism: A Guide to Diagnosis, Intervention, and Treatment.* New York: W.W. Norton.

Geertz, Clifford. 1988. *Works and Lives.* Stanford, Calif.: Stanford University Press.

Geller, Anne. 1983. Alcoholics Anonymous and the Scientific Model. In *Etiologic Aspects of Alcohol and Drug Abuse*, edited by Gottheil et al. Springfield, Ill.: Charles C. Thomas, pp. 306–318.

Gibbons, R. J., Y. Israel, H. Kalant, R. Papham, W. Schmidt, and R. Smart, eds. 1975. *Research Advances in Alcohol and Drug Problems.* New York: John Wiley and Sons.

Goodenough, Ward H. 1990. Evolution of the Human Capacity for Beliefs. *American Anthropologist* 92:597–612.

Goodwin, Donald W. 1983. The Genetics of Alcoholism. In *Etiologic Aspects of Alcohol and Drug Abuse*, edited by Gottheil et al. Springfield, Ill.: Charles C. Thomas, pp. 5–13.

Gordon, Andrew J. 1984. Alcohol Use in the Perspective of Cultural Ecology. In *Recent Developments in Alcoholism*, Vol. 2, edited by M. Galanter. New York: Plenum Press, pp. 355–375.

Gottheil, Edward, Keith A. Druley, Thomas Skoloda, and Howard M. Waxman, eds. 1983. *Etiologic Aspects of Alcohol and Drug Abuse.* Springfield, Ill.: Charles C. Thomas.

Graves, Theodore D. 1967. Acculturation, Access, and Alcohol in Three Ethnic Communities. *American Anthropologist* 69:306–321.

―――. 1970. The Personal Adjustment of Navajo Indian Migrants to Denver, Colorado. *American Anthropologist* 72:35–54.

Gurman, A. S. and A. M. Razim. 1977. *Effective Psychotherapy: A Handbook of Research.* New York: Pergamon Press.

Gusfield, Joseph. 1987. Passage to Play: Rituals of Drinking Time in American Society. In *Constructive Drinking*, edited by M. Douglas. New York: Cambridge University Press, pp. 73–90.

Harris, Grace Gredys. 1989. Mechanism and Morality in Patients' Views of Illness and Injury. *Medical Anthropology Quarterly* NS 3(1):3–21.

Hartford, T. C., and D . A. Parker. 1985. Alcohol, Drugs and Tobacco: An International Perspective, Past, Present, and Future II. *Proceedings of the 34th International Congress on Alcoholism and Drug Abuse.*

Harwood, H. J., P. Kristiansen, and J.V. Rachal. 1985. *Social and Economic Costs of Alcohol Abuse and Alcoholism. Issue Report No. 2.* Research Triangle Park, N.C.: Research Triangle Institute.

Hatch, Elvin. 1973. Social Drinking and Factional Alignment in a Rural California Community. *Anthropology Quarterly* 46:243–260.

Heath, Dwight B. 1958. Drinking Patterns of the Bolivian Camba. *Quarterly Journal of Studies on Alcohol* 19:491–508.

————. 1975. A Critical Review of Ethnographic Studies of Alcohol Use. In *Research Advances in Alcohol and Drug Problems,* Vol. 2, edited by Gibbons et al. New York: John Wiley & Sons, pp. 1–92.

————. 1983. Sociocultural Perspectives on Addiction. In *Etiologic Aspects of Alcohol and Drug Abuse,* edited by Gottheil et al. Springfield, Ill.: Charles C. Thomas, pp. 223–237.

————.1984a. Selected Contexts of Anthropological Studies in the Alcohol Field: Intoduction. In *Recent Developments in Alcoholism,* Vol. 2, edited by M. Galanter. New York: Plenum Press, pp. 377–381.

————.1984b. Cross-Cultural Studies of Alcoholism. In *Recent Developments in Alcoholism,* Vol. 2, edited by M. Galanter. New York: Plenum Press, pp. 405–416.

————.1984c. Comment on Room's Alcohol and Ethnography: A Case of Problem Deflation? *Current Anthopology* 25:180–181.

————.1987a. Anthropology and Alcohol Studies: Current Issues. In *Annual Review of Anthropology,* Vol. 16, edited by Siegel et al. Palo Alto, Calif.: Annual Reviews, pp. 99–142.

————. 1987b. A decade of development in the anthropological study of alcohol use. In *Constructive Drinking: Perspectives on Drink from Anthropology,* edited by M. Douglas. New York: Cambridge University Press, pp. 16–70.

Heath, Dwight B., Jack O. Waddell, and Martin D.Topper, eds. 1981a. Cultural Factors in Alcohol Research and Treatment of Drinking Problems. New Brunswick, N.J.:*Journal of Studies on Alcohol.* Supplement No. 9.

Heath, Dwight B., Jack O. Waddell, and Martin D. Topper, eds. 1981a. *Cultural Factors in Alcohol Research and Treatment of Drinking Problems.* New Brunswick, N.J.: Journal of Studies on Alcohol. Supplement No. 9.

Heather, Nick, and Ian Robertson. 1989. *Problem Drinking.* New York: Oxford University Press.

Hill, Thomas W. 1978. Drunken Comportment of Urban Indians: "Time Out" Behavior? *Journal of Anthropological Research* 34:442–467.

————. 1984. Ethnohistory and Alcohol Studics. In *Recent Developments in Alcoholism,* Vol. 2, edited by M. Galanter. New York: Plenum Press, pp. 313–337.

————. 1990. Peyotism and the Control of Heavy Drinking: The Nebraska Winnebago in the Early 1900's. *Human Organization* 49:255–256.

Hilton, M.E. 1987. Demographic Characteristics and the Frequency of Heavy Drinking as Predictors of Self Reported Drinking Problems. *British Journal of Addiction* 82:913–925.

Hippler, Arthur E. 1974. An Alaskan Athabascan Technique for Overcoming Alcohol Abuse. *Artic* 27:53–67.

Holder, H. D. 1987. Alcohol Treatment and Potential Health Care Cost Savings. *Medical Care* 16:99–142.

Horton, Donald. 1943. The Function of Alcohol in Primitive Societies: A Cross-Cultural Study. *Quarterly Journal of Studies on Alcohol* 4:199.

Imbach, Jeffrey D. 1992. *The Recovery of Love: Christian Mysticism and the Addictive Society.* New York: Crossroad Publishing.

Jarvie, L. C. 1968. Conflict and Congruence in Anthropological Theory. In *Theory in Anthropology: A Sourcebook,* edited by R. A. Manners and D. Kaplan. Chicago: Aldine Publishing.

Jellinek, E.M. 1960. *The Disease Concept of Alcoholism.* New Haven, Conn.: College and University Press.

Jensen, Gary F., Joseph H. Strauss, and Y. William Harris. 1977. Crime, Deliquency, and the American Indian. *Human Organization* 36:252–257.

Johnston, L. D., P. M. O'Malley, and J. G. Bachman. 1988. Illicit Drugs Use: Smoking and Drinking by America's High School Students, College Students and Young Adults. *DHHS* Pub. No.(ADM) 89–1602. Rockville, Md.: ADAMHA.

Johnston, Thomas F. 1973. Musical Instruments and Practices of the Tsonga Beer Drink. *Behavior Science Notes* 8:5.

Kearney, Michael. 1970. Drunkenness and Religious Conversion in a Mexican Village. *Quarterly Journal of Studies on Alcohol* 31:132–152.

————. 1975. World View Theory and Study. In *Annual Review of Anthropology,* Vol. 4, edited by Siegel et al. Palo Alto, Calif.: Annual Reviews, pp. 247–270.

————. 1984. *World View.* Novato, Calif.: Chandler and Sharp.

Kemnitzer, Luis, S. 1972. The Structure of Country Drinking Parties on Pine Ridge Reservation, South Dakota. *Plains Anthropologist* 17:134–142.

Khantzian, E. J. 1990. Self-Regulation and Self-Medication Factors in Alcoholism and the Addictions: Similarities and Differences. In *Recent Developments in Alcoholism,* Vol. 8, edited by M. Galanter. New York: Plenum Press, pp. 255–271.

Khantzian, Edward J., and John E. Mack. 1989. Alcoholics Anonymous and Contemporary Psychodynamic Theory. In *Recent Developments in Alcoholism*, Vol. 7, edited by M. Galanter. New York: Plenum Press, pp. 67–90.

Kissin, B., and H. Begleiter, eds. 1977. *Treatment and Rehabilitation of the Chronic Alcoholic.* New York: Plenum Press.

Klausner, S. Z. 1964. Sacred and Profane Meanings of Blood and Alcohol. *Journal of Social Psychology* 64:27.

Kondo, Dorrine K. 1986. The Dissolution and the Reconstitution of Self: Implications for Anthropological Epistemology. *Cultural Anthropology* 1:74–88.

Kuper, Adam, ed. 1977. *The Social Anthropology of Radcliffe-Brown.* Boston: Routledge and Kegan Paul.

Kurtz, Ernest. 1979. *Not God: A History of Alcoholics Anonymous.* Minneapolis: Hazelden Educational Services.

Leach, B. 1973. Does Alcoholics Anonymous Really Work? In *Alcoholism: Research and Treatment,* edited by P. G. Bourne and R. Fox. New York: Academic Press.

Leach, B., and J. L. Norris. 1977. Factors in the Development of Alcoholics Anonymous. In *Treatment and Rehabilitation of the Chronic Alcoholic,* edited by B. Kissin and H. Begleiter. New York: Plenum Press, pp. 441–543.

Leavitt, Stewart Bruce. 1974. *Social Uses and Communication of Myths in a Rescue Organization: Alcoholics Anonymous,* Unpublished Ph.D. diss. Northwestern University, Speech.

Leland, J. H. 1976. *Firewater Myths: North American Indian Drinking and Alcohol Addiction.* New Brunswick, N.J.: Rutgers Center of Alcohol Studies Monograph 11.

————. 1984. Comment on Room's Alcohol and Ethnography: A Case of Problem Deflation? *Current Anthropology* 25:182.

Levin, Jerome D. 1987. *Treatment of Alcoholism and Other Addictions: A Self-Psychology Approach.* Northvale, N.J.: Jason Aronson.

————. 1990. *Alcoholism: A Bio-Psycho-Social Approach.* New York: Hemisphere Publishing.

Levine, H. G. 1978. The discovery of addiction. *Journal of Studies on Alcohol* 39:143–174.

————. 1984. The Alcohol Problem in America: From Temperance to Alcoholism. *British Journal of Addiction* 79:109–119.

Levinson, David. 1983. Current Status of the Field: An Anthropological Perspective on the Behavior Modification Treatment of Alcoholism. In *Recent Developments in*

*Alcoholis*m, Vol. 1, edited by M. Galanter. New York: Plenum Press, pp. 255–261.

Levy, J. E. 1984. Comment on Room's Alcohol and Ethnography: A Case of Problem Deflation? *Current Anthropology* 25:182.

Levy, Jerrold E., and Everett Kunitz. 1969. Navajo Criminal Homicide. *Southwestern Journal of Anthropology* 25:124–152.

MacAndrew, Craig, and Robert B. Edgerton. 1969. *Drunken Comportment: A Social Explanation*. Chicago: Aldine Publishing.

Madsen, William. 1974. *The American Alcoholic: The Nature-Nuture Controversy in Alcoholic Research and Therapy*. Springfield, Ill.: Charles C. Thomas.

———. 1979. Alcoholics Anonymous as a Crisis Cult. In *Beliefs, Behaviors and Alcoholic Beverages*, edited by M. Marshall. Ann Arbor: University of Michigan Press, pp. 382–387.

———. 1984. Comment on Room's Alcohol and Ethnography: A Case of Problem Deflation? *Current Anthropology* 25:183.

Maida, Carl A. 1984. Social Network Considerations in the Alcohol Field. In *Recent Developments in Alcoholism*, Vol. 2, edited by M. Galanter. New York: Plenum Press, pp. 339–353.

Malinowski, Bronislaw. 1944. *A Scientific Theory of Culture and Other Essays*. Chapel Hill: University of North Carolina Press.

Mandelbaum, David G. 1965. Alcohol and Culture. *Current Anthropolgy* 6:281–293.

Mangin, William. 1957. Drinking Among Andean Indians. *Quarterly Journal of Studies on Alcohol* 18:55–65.

Manners, R. A., and D. Kaplan. 1968. *Theory in Anthropology: A Sourcebook*. Chicago: Aldine Publishing.

Manning, Frank E. 1977. The Salvation of a Drunk. *American Ethnologist* 4:379–412.

Marlatt, G. A., J. S. Baer, D. M. Donovan, and D. R. Kivlahan. 1988. Addictive Behaviors: Etiology and Treatment. *Annual Review of Pschology* 39:223–252.

Marrus, Francine Elizabeth. 1988. *A Way Back to Life: Descriptions and Discoveries About the Role of Communication in the Enculturation Performance of Alcoholics Anonymous*. Unpublished Ph.D. diss. Ohio University. Speech Communication.

Marshall, Mac. 1980. Alcohol and Culture: A Review. *Alcohol Health and Research World* 4(4): 417–432.

———. 1984. Comment on Room's Alcohol and Ethnography: A Case of Problem Deflation? *Current Anthropology* 25:184.

———, ed. 1979. *Beliefs, Behaviors, and Alcoholic Beverages: A Cross-Cultural Survey*. Ann Arbor: University of Michigan Press.

Marvel, B. 1993. Alcohol and Youth. *Dallas Morning News*. May 25, p. C-6.

May, Phillip A. 1977. Explanations of Native American Drinking: A Review. *Plains Anthropologist* 22:223–232.

McClelland, D. C., W. N. Davis, R. Kalin, and Eric Wanner. 1972. *The Drinking Man*. New York: The Free Press.

McLure, Charles E., Jr., and Wayne R. Thirsk. 1978. The Inequity of Taxing Iniquity: A Plea for Reduced Sumptuary Taxes in Developing Countries. *Economic Development and Cultural Change* 26:487–504.

Moos, Rudolf H., John W. Finney, and Ruth C. Cronkite. 1990. *Alcoholism Treatment: Context, Process, and Outcome*. New York: Oxford University Press.

Mulkern, V., and R. Spence. 1984. *Alcohol Abuse/Alcoholism among Homeless Persons: A Review of the Literature*. Final Report. Washington, D.C.: U.S. Goverment Printing Office.

Nagel, George, Jr. 1988. *Identity Reconstruction: Communication and Story Telling in*

Alcoholics Anonymous. Unpublished Ph.D. diss. University of Utah. Speech Communication.

Narayan, Kirin. 1993. How Native Is a "Native" Anthropologist? *American Anthropologist* 95:671–686.

National Institute on Alcohol Abuse and Alcoholism (NIAAA). 1990. *Seventh Special Report to the Congress on Alcohol and Health.* Washington, D.C.: Secretary of Health and Human Sciences.

Ogborne, A. C., and F. B. Glaser. 1981. Characteristics of Affiliates of Alcoholics Anonymous. *Quarterly Journal of Studies on Alcohol* 42:661–675.

Ogborne, Alan C. 1989. Some Limitations of Alcoholics Anonymous. In *Recent Developments in Alcoholism*, Vol. 7, edited by M. Galanter. New York: Plenum Press, pp. 55–66.

O'Leary, M. R., D. A. Calsyn, D. L. Haddock, and C.W. Freeman. 1980. Differential Alcohol Use Patterns and Personality Traits among Three Alcoholics Anonymous Attendance Level Groups: Further Consideration of the Affiliation Profile. *Drug and Alcohol Dependence* 5:35–144.

O'Reilly, Edmund Bernard. 1988. *Toward Rhetorical Immunity: Narratives of Alcoholism and Recovery.* Unpublished Ph.D. diss. University of Pennsylvania. Folklore.

Ossenberg, Richard J. 1969. Social Class and Bar Behavior During an Urban Festival. *Human Organization* 28:29–34.

Patrick, Clarence H. 1952. *Alcohol, Culture, and Society.* Durham, N.C.: Duke University Press.

Pattison, E. M., M. B. Sobell, and L. C. Sobell. 1977. *Emerging Concepts of Alcohol Dependence.* New York: Springer.

Polich, J. M., D. J. Armor, and H. B. Braiker. 1980. *The Course of Alcoholism: Four Years After Treatment.* Santa Monica, Calif.: Rand Corporation.

Query, William T., and Joy M. Query. 1972. Aggressive Responses to the Holtzman Inkblot Technique by Indian and White Alcoholics. *Journal of Crosscultural Psychology* 3(4): 413–416.

Radcliffe-Brown, A. 1952. *Structure and Function in Primitive Society.* New York: The Free Press.

Robbins, Michael C. 1977. Problem Drinking and the Integration of Alcohol in Rural Buganda. *Medical Anthropology* 1:1–24.

Robbins, Richard Howard. 1973. Alcohol and the Identity Struggle: Some Effects of Economic Change on Interpersonal Relations. *American Anthropologist* 75:99–122.

Robertson, Nan. 1988. *Getting Better: Inside Alcoholics Anonymous.* New York: William Morrow and Company.

Rodin, M. B. 1981. Alcoholism as a Folk Disease: The Paradox of Beliefs and Choice of Therapy in an Urban American Community. *Journal of Studies on Alcohol* 42:822–835.

Room, Robin. 1984. Alcohol and Ethnography: A Case of Problem Deflation? *Current Anthropology* 25:169–191.

Room, Robin, and James F. Mosher. 1979. Out of the Shadow of Treatment: A Role for Regulatory Agencies in the Prevention of Alcohol Problems. *Alcohol Health and Research World* 4(2): 248–68.

Rozien, J. 1982. *Estimating Alcohol Involvement in Serious Events.* National Institute of Alcohol Abuse and Alcoholism: Alcohol Consumptions and Related Problems. Alcohol and Health Monograph No. 1. DHHS Pub. No. (ADM) 82-1190. Washington, D.C.: U.S. Government Printing Office, pp.179–219.

Rubington, Earl. 1968. The Bottle Gang. *Quarterly Journal of Studies on Alcohol* 29:943–955.

Rychtarick, R., J. Fairbank, C. Allen, D. Foy, and R. Drabman. 1983. Alcohol Use in Television Programming: Effects on Children's Behavior. *Addictive Behavior* 8:19–22.

Sadler, Patricia O. 1977. The "Crisis Cult" as a Voluntary Association: An Interactional Approach to Alcoholics Anonymous. *Human Organization* 36:207–210.

Sayres, William C. 1956. Ritual Drinking, Ethnic Studies, and Inebriety in Rural Colombia. *Quarterly Journal of Studies on Alcohol* 17:53–62.

Schael, Anne Wilson. 1986. *When a Society Hits Bottom: The American Culture as Addict (Addictions, Social Change, Paradigm)*. Unpublished Ph.D. diss. Union for Experimenting Colleges/Union without Walls and Union Graduate School. Psychology.

Service, Elman R. 1962. *Primitive Social Organization*. New York: Random House.

Simmons, Ozzie G. 1959. Drinking Patterns and Interpersonal Performance in a Peruvian Mestizo Community. *Quarterly Journal of Studies on Alcohol* 20:103–111.

Smith, Annette R. 1991. *Alcoholics Anonymous: A Social World Perspective*. Unpublished Ph.D. diss. University of California at San Diego. Sociology.

Smith, Stephen Richard. 1988. *Drinking and Sobriety in Japan*. Unpublished Ph.D. diss. Columbia University. Anthropology.

Sobell, M. B., and L. C. Sobell. 1973. Individualized Behavior Therapy for Alcoholics. *Behavior Therapy* 4:49–72.

Sournia, Jean Charles. 1990. *A History of Alcoholism*. Oxford: Basil Blackwell.

Spindler, George D., and Louise Spindler. 1983. Anthropologists View American Culture. In *Annual Review of Anthropology*, Vol. 12, edited by Siegel et al. Palo Alto, Calif.: Annual Reviews, pp. 49–78.

Spradley, J. P. 1970. *You Owe Yourself a Drunk: An Ethnography of Urban Nomads*. Boston: Little, Brown and Company.

Spradley, J. P., and B. J. Mann. 1975. *The Cocktail Waitress: Woman's Work in a Man's World*. New York: John Wiley and Sons.

Steward, Julian. 1968. Levels of Sociocultural Integration: An Operational Concept. In *Theory in Anthropology: A Sourcebook*, edited by R. A. Manners and D. Kaplan. Chicago: Aldine Publishing.

Strenski, Ivan, ed. 1992. *Malinowswki and the Work of Myth*. Princeton N.J.: Princeton University Press.

Strug, David L. 1981. Anthropological Research: Its Relevance to the Treatment of Alcoholism and Drug Addictions. *Journal of Studies on Alcohol* 42:819–821.

Strug, D. L., and M. M. Hyman. 1981. Social Networks of Alcoholics. *Journal of Studies on Alcohol* 42:855–884.

Strug, David L., S. Priyadarsini, and Merton M. Hyman, eds. 1986. *Alcohol Interventions: Historical and Sociocultural Approaches*. New York: The Haworth Press.

Swartz, Theodore, and Lola Romanucci-Ross. 1974. Drinking and Inebriate Behavior in the Admiralty Islands, Melanesia. *Ethos* 2:213–231.

Tarter, Ralph E. 1983. The Causes of Alcoholism: A Biopsycological Analysis. In *Etiologic Aspects of Alcohol and Drug Abuse*, edited by Gottheil et al. Springfield, Ill.: Charles C. Thomas, pp. 173–201.

Tarter, Ralph E., and A. Arthur Sugerman. 1976. *An Interdisciplinary Approach to Alcoholism*. Reading, Mass.: Addison-Wesley.

Tedlock, Barbara. 1991. From Participant Observation to the Observation of Particpation: The Emergence of Narrative Ethnography. *Journal of Anthropological Research* 47:69–94.

Thoreson, Richard W., and Frank C. Budd. 1987. Self-Help Groups Procedures for Treating Alcohol Problems. In *Treatment and Prevention of Alcohol Problems*, edited by W. Miles Cox. New York: Academic Press, pp. 157–183.

Topper, Martin 1981. The Drinker's Story. In *Cultural Factors in Alcohol Research and Treatment of Drinking Problems,* edited by Heath et al. New Brunswick, N.J.: Journal of Studies on Alcohol. Supplement No. 9.

Trice, H. M. 1957. A Study of the Process of Affiliation with Alcoholics Anonymous. *Quarterly Journal of Studies on Alcohol* 18:39–54.

———. 1959. The Affiliative Motive and Readiness to Join Alcoholics Anonymous. *Quarterly Journal of Studies on Alcohol* 20:313–321.

Trice, H. M., and P. M. Roman. 1970. Sociological Predictors of Affiliation with Alcoholics Anonymous. *Social Psychiatry* 5:51–59.

Trice, Harrison M., and William J. Staudenmeier. 1989. A Sociocultural History of Alcoholics Anonymous. In *Recent Developments in Alcoholism,* Vol. 7, edited by M. Galanter. New York: Plenum Press, pp. 11–35.

Turnbull, C. M. 1972. *The Mountain People.* New York: Simon and Schuster.

Turner, Victor 1975. Symbolic Studies. In *Annual Review of Anthropology*, Vol. 4, edited by Siegel et al. Palo Alto, Calif.: Annual Reviews, pp. 145–57.

Vaillant, George E. 1983. *The Natural History of Alcoholism.* Cambridge, Mass.: Harvard University Press.

Van der Geest, Sjaak, and Susan Reynolds Whyte. 1989. The Charm of Medicines: Metaphors and Metonyms. *Medical Anthropology Quarterly* (n.s.) 3:345–367.

Van Natta, P., H. Malin, D. Bertolucci, and C. Kaelber. 1984–85. The Hidden Influence of Alcohol on Mortality. *Epidemiologic Bulletin No. 6. Alcohol Health and Research World* 9:42–45.

Waddell, Jack O. 1983. The Alcoholic Patient as an Ethnographic Domain: The Anthropologist's Role in the Therapeutic Process. *Journal of Studies on Alcohol* 42:846–855.

———. 1984. Alcoholism-Treatment-Center-Based Projects. In *Recent Developments in Alcoholism*, Vol. 2, edited by M. Galanter. New York: Plenum Press, pp. 397–404.

Wallace, John 1983. Ideology, Belief and Behavior: Alcoholics Anonymous as a Social Movement. In *Etiologic Aspects of Alcohol and Drug Abuse*, edited by Gottheil et al. Springfield, Ill.: Charles C. Thomas, pp. 285–305.

Wallack, L., W. Breed, and J. Cruz. 1987. Alcohol on Prime Time Television. *Journal of Studies on Alcohol* 48:33–38.

Westermeyer, Joseph. 1984. Cross-Cultural Aspects of Alcoholism in the Elderly. In *Recent Developments in Alcoholism,* Vol. 2, M. Galanter, ed. New York: Plenum Press, pp. 289–301.

Woodruff, D., ed. 1976. A Brief Method of Screening for Alcoholism. *Diseases of the Nervous System* 37:434–435.

Wright, J. D., J. W. Knight, E. Weber-Burdin, and J. Lam. 1987. Ailments and Alcohol: Health Status Among the Drinking Homeless. *Alcohol Health and Research World* 11:22–27.

Index

About the Author

DANNY M. WILCOX is Adjunct Professor of Anthropology, Institute of Anthropology, School of Community Service at the University of North Texas. He authored the chapter "Drug Culture: Everybody Uses Something" in Larry L. Naylor, ed., *Cultural Diversity in the United States* (Bergin & Garvey, 1997).

ISBN 0-275-96049-8

90000>

EAN

9 780275 960490

HARDCOVER BAR CODE